THE ASHES
SURRENDERED

THE ASHES SURRENDERED

The **Guardian** BOOK OF THE 1989 ASHES SERIES

MIKE SELVEY

Macdonald
Queen Anne Press

A *Queen Anne Press* BOOK

© Mike Selvey 1989

First published in Great Britain in 1989 by
Queen Anne Press, a division of
Macdonald & Co (Publishers) Ltd
66–73 Shoe Lane
London
EC4P 4AB

A member of Maxwell Pergamon Publishing Corporation plc

All photographs by Graham Morris

Jacket photographs – Front: Steve Waugh/Jack Russell, Old Trafford Test match, 1989
Back: David Gower, Lord's Test match, 1989

Scoreboards compiled by Wendy Wimbush

Design – Deborah Holmes

British Library Cataloguing in Publication Data
Selvey, Mike
    The Ashes Surrendered, 1989.
    1. Cricket. English teams. Test matches with Australian teams. Trophies
I. Title
796.35'865
ISBN 0–356–18672–5

Typeset, printed and bound in Great Britain by
Butler & Tanner Ltd, Frome, Somerset

CONTENTS

Prologue

'O brave new world, that has such people in't' – The Tempest

There is, it would be fair to say, nothing in sport to compare with the Ashes. It is 107 years now since England, chasing a mere 85 to beat Billy Murdoch's Australians; collapsed on a drying pitch from 51 for 2 to 77 all out, so giving Albert 'Monkey' Hornby the doubtful distinction of being the first captain to lose to Australia on English soil.

So stunned was the nation at the indignity that a young journalist, Reginald Brooks, felt compelled to write the twee Victorian prankster's obituary – 'in affectionate remembrance of English cricket, which died at the Oval, 29th August 1882' – which appeared in the *Sporting Times*. 'The body will be cremated and the Ashes taken to Australia.' He knew not what he had started. Brooks died six years later; today, permanently on display in the museum at Lord's sits the small, singularly unimposing urn which is testament to his joke.

How it came into existence is debatable. Three weeks after the Oval defeat, the Hon. Ivo Bligh sailed for Australia with a side – the trip had been planned before the defeat – whose avowed intention now was to 'recover the Ashes'. By winning the last two of three Tests, he achieved the spiritual recovery, but it was given substance when, so it was said, a group of Melbourne women presented him with the urn containing the remains of the bails used in the match. Subsequent evidence suggests that it came not from

Australian ladies but Sir William Clarke, and contains the detritus of a cricket ball.

No matter; the legend was born. Since that day, men have given blood in pursuit of the absurd trophy, war has almost been declared, the rules and spirit of the game stretched at times to the absolute limit and beyond, not for the tangible spoils of sporting warfare (the right to raise a trophy totemistically high in victory) but for the ideal of the competition, the fiercest, most nationalistic, jingoistic in the business.

It is also a feature of the Ashes that no matter how poor the respective strengths of the two sides may be, the competition will always be fierce. It matters not, they would say in Australia, if you are beaten by West Indies or Pakistan. And although it would be undesirable if Sri Lanka were to get the better of you, that would not be the end of the world. But don't bother coming home if the Poms do you. Before this summer, there have been 54 'Clashes for the Ashes' as the marketing men have come to calling them. At the end of them, the Ashes have ended up in English hands on 28 occasions and 26 times they have gone to Australia; it's as close as that.

Allan Border, a supreme batsman, arrived in England in May with an unedifying prospect ahead of him. In 1981, he had toured England under Kim Hughes and had watched a position of strength disintegrate and crumble as Ian

Botham carried all before him. It was a set-back that has haunted Australians ever since, for although Greg Chappell temporarily restored the seat of power to Australia when he beat Bob Willis's side two winters later, the 1985 series in England, with Border now captain, was a massacre. In 1986–87 the deed was compounded when Mike Gatting triumphed against him in Australia. Now Border, captain for the third time, faced the real prospect of becoming the only captain in Ashes history to lose three series in a row.

Yet curiously, that 1985 walloping, and the one by Gatting, may just have served as the catalyst Australia needed to rebuild a side that had been hampered – just as it had been immediately pre- and post-Packer – by the clandestine atmosphere surrounding the recruitment of a rebel tour to South Africa and its subsequent effect on morale. Border, who for those years virtually carried the Australian batting, time after time poddling to the crease in a crisis and keeping honour afloat, and Bobby Simpson together began to plan the revival. They would go for young players to mix with hard experience and they would back them. The would look for good basic techniques and hone them. They would back their judgement, and be prepared for short-term failures in pursuit of ultimate success. The first glimmer came one early evening two years ago in Calcutta when, against the odds, Border and Australia beat Gatting's England to steal the World Cup from under Pakistani and Indian noses. Last winter, after a fearful towel-ling from West Indies, they stemmed the flow with a win and a creditable draw in the last two matches. Border's side was coming of age.

For England by contrast, these past few years have steadily brought blacker and blacker times, When Border was last here with Australia, his final deed of the series was to stand on the Oval balcony and watch David Gower, the England captain, self-consciously raise a replica of the Ashes urn to the crowd spread out on the turf below. If for Border that moment had hurt beyond measure, for England it seemed to herald the start of an era of good times. The record is to the contrary. From that day until the start of this summer, England lost series both home and away to West Indies and Pakistan, and also lost at home to India and New Zealand. Only Gat-ting's Australian tour was a success, with two Tests being won. Just a solitary win at Lord's last year, in a one-off game against Sri Lanka, has since then broken the most dismal period in English Test history.

Captains have come and gone: Gower was dumped at Lord's in unceremonious and cow-ardly fashion by the chairman of the English selectors, Peter May, following defeat by India. Gatting, after his Australian triumph the fol-lowing winter became increasingly petulant, pre-siding over and even condoning ill-discipline. In Pakistan he had a run-in with an umpire which threatened to end the tour; the following summer he was sacked after allegations unbecoming to his position of impropriety with a barmaid. John Emburey lasted two tests, and Chris Cowdrey one, before injury, looked on it seemed as an expedient by the selectors, propelled him back to the ranks forever.

Graham Gooch was given one Test, but it sowed the seeds for the gaffe of all gaffes per-petrated in May's seven years in charge. In 1982, during England's tour to India, Gooch had played a major role in setting up a rebel England tour to South Africa which took place the fol-lowing spring and which he captained. Gooch and the other tourists received a three-year ban from Test matches, but on his return to the Test arena he experienced hostility, particularly in West Indies. But Gooch had become an increas-ingly reluctant tourist and with England sched-uled to visit India again last winter, he had signed a contract to play cricket for Western Province in South Africa instead. It therefore came as a shock to find that not only was Gooch going to India, but that he would be captain. Indeed, one seemed conditional on the other.

The reaction was predictable. Although India had received Gooch without protest during the World Cup, they had understood that he would not be going back to South Africa. Furthermore, it was discovered that Gooch had had to obtain permission from Western Province to break his contract to play there. This proved a bit much for them, and with a bid – unsuccessful as it turned out – for the Commonwealth games to protect, India let it be known that all England tourists who featured on the UN blacklist would be refused entry visas. The tour foundered, and so, in spite of stringent efforts by the Test and County Cricket Board to get cricket at all costs when a break would have been better, did the winter.

But from it all, a silver lining appeared. An opportunity had presented itself not only for the players to have a complete break from the year round slog that international cricket has become, but for those who run the game to sit back and take stock.

English cricket, unwanted in any part of the world (save South Africa), had to revise its thinking. Then several things happened. First of all, Peter May resigned as chairman of selectors. Then in January, in a move to prevent the fragmentation of world cricket, the International Cricket Conference, of which TCCB is, of course, a part, reached a unanimous and far-reaching decision to ban from Test cricket for a minimum of four years any player who coached or played cricket in South Africa after April 1st 1989, with the proviso, though, that there would be an amnesty for all cricketers who had been there before that date.

It meant, in the eyes of many – players, administrators and public alike – that a future existed in which stability, however precarious, would play its part. But who should lead England into this brave new world? The TCCB had no doubts. Amid the sort of publicity that is the man's stock in trade as a PR consultant, Ted Dexter was invited not only to be chairman of selectors, but to head a newly formed England committee whose brief was to rethink and implement a complete restructuring of the English game from Test level down to grassroots. Tests, as Dexter saw it, were important, but only the tip of the iceberg, and a system had to be found whereby talent could be identified at an early age and transplanted into the best possible environment to bring it swiftly to fruition. Furthermore Dexter, for obvious reasons obliged to give up a lucrative sideline with the Sunday Mirror, was, amid some controversy, to become the first paid chairman by way of recompense.

Dexter is, and always has been a high-profile person; former England Captain, wonderfully natural attacking batsman, top-flight amateur golfer, pilot, racer of greyhounds, lover of fast cars and motorbikes, television pundit and occasional writer of pulp fiction. He is also easily bored. But against that, he is a pretty shrewd theorist on the game.

His first decision would be to appoint a captain for presumably the summer, and despite pressure to reinstate Gatting, he instead went unhesitatingly for Gower, a man whose natural skills, articulate bearing, and love of champagne and the Cresta Run fit very closely into his own image. The marriage was applauded. England would prove invincible. Good times were just around the corner.

On the face of it then, Allan Border was remarkably good-humoured when he unveiled his touring party at a West London hotel. The last thing you need after flying halfway round the world and arriving five hours late is to exchange banalities with the suitably fed and sponsored media assembled to greet you. 'Pleased to be here, Allan? ... D'you think you can win? ... Is it important to you? ... Looking forward to playing against Ian Botham? ...' The questions rolled on; the eyes, travel-bleary, just rolled. It was enough to drive anyone to jet-lag, but Border, on auto-pilot and surrounded by his boys, fielded everything. All was sweetness and light. Bobby Simpson, the assistant manager, shook hands with the man from the *Sun*, and said how pleased he was to see him (look forward to the return match in September). Back home, Border, miffed by the never-ending grind of such press meetings, had acquired a reputation for brusqueness. 'Ask him about the Captain Cranky stories,' came a mischievous prompt. No one dared.

Border in fact exuded confidence, and felt that the team gathered round him, whispering asides to each other, was more than capable of winning the Ashes. And in view of past experiences, yes, victory would be all the more sweet if Ian Botham were playing.

He carries with him, though, a side almost totally lacking experience of English Test match conditions. Apart from himself, only Terry Alderman, David Boon and Geoff Lawson have toured before, Alderman not since 1981. Against that, however, Border (with Essex), Alderman (at, first of all, Kent and then Gloucester) and Steve Waugh (brilliantly at Somerset last season) have all had valuable county experience. Border's is double-edged, for he makes no secret of the fact that he has picked the brains of Keith Fletcher, one of the shrewdest of modern captains.

Around him, there is a nucleus of potentially good, correct batsmen. No need to mention Border further, but Geoff Marsh, Border's vice-captain, and Boon have welded together into a formidable and prolific opening pair, although there is curious talk of the left-hander Mark Taylor splitting them up. Dean Jones is a precocious talent and has scored two Test double-centuries already, and Waugh, without a century at all yet, will surely rectify that before long. Tom Moody, tall and powerful, and Mike Veletta, dapper and perky, complete the list. The wicket-keeping will be shared by Ian Healy and Tim Zoehrer, the former in the Tests and the latter no doubt in the one-day stuff.

But if Border is to make headway, it will be his bowlers who do it. Last time he was here, he had no control as England rampaged through the series. This time it may be different. He has two spinners: Tim May, an off-spinner who will shred his fingers in an effort to find turn, and Trevor Hohns, a leg-spinner restored to the side after serving a ban for going with the rebel Australians to South Africa.

Spin won't play much of a part, though, and Border has brought five seamers to do the job. While Border was introducing his side to the media, all the attention was focusing on a large moustache with a cricketer somewhere behind it, and probably an agent behind that. Merv Hughes has become a 'character' ever since he blustered his way to a hat-trick and 13 wickets against West Indies at Perth last winter. He is reputed to be a reformed rouster, who has foresaken the demon drink for a year in the cause. How much good it's done him is hard to judge; take away Perth and he has a Test bowling average of around 60. Border wants him to be the man we love to hate. But he won't win the Ashes for him. Nor will Carl Rackemann, another rebel returned to the fold, who is quick but mighty unreliable, or young Greg Campbell, a 'Neighbours' lookalike who is here for the experience of a lifetime and much donkey work.

As Border spoke, away out of the glare of television lights, and smiling nudgingly and knowingly at the Merv Ballyhoo, stood Alderman and Lawson. They have seen it all, and Border will pack them in cottonwool to get them through the series. For Australia, they are the key.

PART ONE

Texaco Trophy One-Day Series

First Texaco Trophy One-Day International

England v Australia
Old Trafford, 25 May 1989

England 231–9
Australia 136 all out
England won by 95 runs

Whatever David Gower or Allan Border may say they feel about the psychological advantages or otherwise of winning the pre-Test one-day series, it is indisputably no positive disadvantage to morale to be one up rather than the reverse. That England, by dint of what was ultimately an embarrassingly easy 95-run win before a packed Old Trafford, are in the former position is due almost entirely to Gower's bowlers who, on a pitch which demanded discipline, control and expertise, produced just that and successfully defended 231.

This was not an insignificant score for a side having chosen to take first knock, but none-theless it was well short of what it ought to have been, following the vibrant flyer given to England by Gooch and Gower, and for Australia it seemed a perfectly gettable target. But once three wickets had fallen in the first nine overs of their reply, with just 17 runs on the board, Australia had their backs to the wall. Steve Waugh (35) and Tom Moody (24) tried, and Geoff Marsh, who opened with David Boon, spent 29 overs of obduracy for his 17, including, while the castle was crumbling around his ears, an interminable time bogged down – forgive me – on one run.

But England's bowling was relentless and the fielding, until late but inconsequential misses by Mike Gatting and Steve Rhodes, high class. Marsh was a victim of Rhodes's acrobatic alertness, Waugh holed out to deep mid-wicket, and the rest was a procession with the last six wickets falling abjectly for 72 runs. Fittingly, the wickets were shared about: three for both Foster and Emburey, who for all his failings in Tests can still be a master of attritional defence in one-day games; a pair, Boon and Waugh, for DeFreitas, and one each for Pringle and Botham, who was rock-steady with not a muck-about ball in sight.

Clive Lloyd, who was the Man of the Match adjudicator, decided that DeFreitas's contribution had been the decisive one, and there may be something in that. In his second over, Boon failed to treat what was a good-length but intrinsically harmless delivery with respect. Instead he drove expansively, missed and saw his off-stump snapped from the ground and cartwheeled gymnastically to the keeper. Now Boon has been in such contemptuous form thus far in the tour that he must believe he can tread the Tasman with impunity. If not the whole recipe, this may have been an ingredient in his dismissal, for in poorer form a little caution would have been the order of the day and his defence would perhaps have kept the ball out.

Instead, the stroke-play of Dean Jones, helmeted now after his recent cheekbone fracture, was exposed to the new ball and after one delightful on-drive, he touched a leg-side delivery from Foster to the keeper. Two overs later Foster produced one from the top drawer to get rid of Border, and Australia were on the run.

One-day cricket, though, if played properly, is a defensive game, and the professionalism of England's bowlers made for deadly dull fare. We can be grateful then for the first three-quarters of an hour of the match, for if we wait all summer there will be nothing more pleasing than the sight of Gower assuming his captain's crown with a blissful innings of 36 from only 33 balls.

There may have been tension in the air at the start. The build-up to the series has been almost overpowering, and certainly Geoff Lawson, for example, although an old hand, looked strung to concert pitch; but Gower rose above it. He drifted Alderman dreamily to the mid-off boundary, picked him delicately behind square and then turned to Lawson, driving him square with as close to savagery as Gower can get. Lawson adjusted his length: Gower rocked back like a lullaby and lifted him over square leg for six as if wafting a bad smell from under his nose.

With Gooch ticking, it was sublime, heady stuff, and 50 came in 10 overs. It could not last. Border, whose bowling changes for a while during the innings proved so instantly productive that it was hard to see why he did not make one every over, brought on Carl Rackemann. The killjoy immediately slanted one across Gower, who edged to Healy.

Everything thereafter paled by contrast. Gatting came and boomed a catch to cover with the aid of Semtex pads – Boon, who caught him,

Scoreboard from Old Trafford

England won toss

England

	6s	4s	Mins	Balls
G A Gooch c Jones b Border.........	52	–	4	134	111
D I Gower c Healy b Rackemann ...	36	1	5	49	33
M W Gatting c Boon b Waugh.......	3	–	–	20	12
A J Lamb b Lawson	35	–	–	80	59
R A Smith c and b Alderman.........	35	–	4	41	40
I T Botham c Boon b Lawson.........	4	–	–	9	12
D R Pringle lbw b Waugh	9	–	–	40	18
†S J Rhodes b Lawson....................	8	–	–	16	16
P A J DeFreitas not out.................	17	–	–	33	20
J E Emburey b Rackemann.............	10	–	–	14	11
N A Foster not out.........................	5	–	–	4	3
Extras (lb 12, w 3, nb 2)..............	17				
Total (9 wkts, 55 overs)	**231**				

FALL OF WICKETS: 1–55, 2–70, 3–125, 4–161, 5–167, 6–179, 7–190, 8–203, 9–220.
BOWLING: Alderman 11–2–38–1 (nb 1); Lawson 11–1–48–3 (w 1); Rackemann 10–1–33–2 (nb 1); Waugh 11–1–45–2 (nb 3, w 2); Moody 8–0–37–0; Border 4–0–18–1.

Australia

	6s	4s	Mins	Balls
G R Marsh c Rhodes b Emburey....	17	–	1	92	78
D C Boon b DeFreitas	5	–	–	13	9
D M Jones c Rhodes b Foster.........	4	–	1	14	15
*A R Border b Foster	4	–	1	7	6
S R Waugh c Smith b DeFreitas.....	35	–	2	81	74
T M Moody b Emburey	24	–	–	43	38
M R J Veletta lbw b Pringle............	17	–	1	32	31
†I A Healy c Emburey b Foster.......	10	–	1	22	20
G F Lawson c DeFreitas b Emburey	0	–	–	2	1
C G Rackemann b Botham	6	–	–	20	9
T M Alderman not out....................	0	–	–	2	2
Extras (b 1, lb 9, w 4).................	14				
Total (47.1 overs)	**136**				

FALL OF WICKETS: 1–8, 2–13, 3–17, 4–64, 5–85, 6–115, 7–119, 8–120, 9–136.
BOWLING: Foster 10–3–29–3 (w 2); DeFreitas 8–3–19–2; Pringle 8–2–19–1 (w 1); Botham 10.1–2–28–1 (w 1); Emburey 11–0–31–3.

Man of the Match: P A J DeFreitas.

Umpires: J W Holder and N T Plews

had done the same thing earlier in the week against Middlesex – and Gooch, when well poised after a thoughtful half-century, disappointingly swept at what should have been the penultimate ball of the morning from Border and top-edged to short fine leg. Shades of Gatting's ill-fated reverse sweep in the World Cup final in Calcutta eighteen months ago.

Arm raised in triumph, DeFreitas bowls Boon to put England in charge at Old Trafford

Joy for Foster and England (BELOW) as Border loses his off stump (LEFT) – but victory at Old Trafford would prove to be England's only success of the summer

The only other innings of substance came from Lamb, who worked the ball around busily for his 35, and Smith, who hit four boundaries in a similar score. But with Lawson regaining his composure to remove Lamb, Botham and Rhodes at a cost of 15, and Waugh and Alderman probing out Smith and Pringle, England tailed away. From 161 for 3, with 15 overs still to bat, a springboard from which they might reasonably have expected to make something in the region of 250, they instead lost six wickets for 70. Not a boundary did they hit during the final dozen overs.

But any hope this must have given Australia was dashed by England's bowlers. Whatever designer drink they imbibe these days instead of beer, Gower will surely have found a vat-ful for them.

Second Texaco Trophy One-Day International

England v Australia
Trent Bridge, 27 May 1989

England 226–5
Australia 226–8
Match Tied

'At the roots of all drama,' so the saying goes, 'farce is to be found' and those who witnessed the tempestuous closing overs of Saturday's second one-day international would be hard pushed to disagree. Australia, chasing a target of 227, and needing a win to keep the three-match series alive, were, in spite of themselves, inching their way home, and arrived at the 55th and final over requiring seven runs with three wickets in hand.

Phil DeFreitas, the bowler, immediately helped the Australian cause by sending down a wide – six runs now from six balls. The batsmen, Ian Healy and Tim May squeezed three singles and a leg-bye from the next four balls, before, with two needed now, May heaved for glory when a nudge might have been better and lost his off-stump.

So with one ball to go, Australia required one to tie, two to win: Gower, as he later admitted, having seen the game drifting away from him earlier, would under the circumstances, have been happy with the tie, but still set a field to stop not the two but the single. DeFreitas missed Carl Rackemann's off stump by a whisker, Steve Rhodes shied at the stumps and missed and the Australian batsmen, who, judging by their subsequent bat-windmilling delight also appeared content with the tie, scampered – well, hobbled, as we shall find out – through for one run. It was the first time that England had been involved in a tie in a one-day international, and only the fourth occasion in all.

There was a vicious sting though as far as Australia were concerned. The competition rules state that should Australia win the final match at Lord's on Monday, and so square the series, England will, in the interests only of deciding who has to polish the trophy, be declared winners of the second match by virtue of having lost fewer wickets. England then, thanks to the existence of a messy retrospective expedient, are the winners of this year's trophy no matter what happens at Lord's. Better, as Gower said, to make sure that the arbitration isn't needed.

But that was only the final act in the farce. The biggest rib-tickler of all had its roots three overs earlier when Steve Waugh and Healy were winning the match for Australia. With 24 still needed, Healy turned Foster to fine leg and scuttled two. Meanwhile Gooch had stopped the boundary and was shaping to throw. Waugh, running to the danger end, was making ground comfortably, only to find Healy dithering outside his crease, ball-watching. He finally sensed Waugh coming at him, turned sharply to set off, twisting his knee in the process and fell back into his crease. With the ball now in the bowler's hands Waugh had to go.

Two overs later Healy, in obvious discomfort, called for a runner and Dean Jones appeared.

Healy promptly drove Foster, and not only ran two, but actually made it faster than his runner. 'He made,' felt Gower, 'an error tactically in haring off like Ben Johnson as soon as his runner came in. Although he was obviously injured, it was not a convincing Oscar performance, and there was some doubt as to whether he was playing the game.' The umpires obviously felt that he wasn't, and gave Jones the red card. 'Nice to see you; thanks for coming,' said Gower.

Cock-ups like that have happened a thousand times before, are certainly not cheating, and in this case resulted from pumping adrenalin and confusion under pressure. Only once before in my experience has a runner been banished, when Ian Gould, then of Middlesex, got his marching orders after similar confusion. But even that was at the instigation of the batsman, Mike Smith, who although handicapped by a severely bleeding nose, said he'd rather bleed to death, thank you.

Since the umpires regarded Jones's presence as surplus to requirements because of Healy's demonstrated speed, they sent him off on appeal by England. Border said later that he would have been 'disappointed' to hear that Gower had interfered, but Jones was able to put his mind at rest on that score. You can bet that some of the other big guns were rumbling though and Dickie Bird and Jack Hampshire should, in spite of any such promptings from crowd or players (the pressure was on England in the field too, don't forget), have had the nous to recognize the situation for what it was, and that Healy was indeed injured – badly enough to have the knee put in a brace later, and, with the other keeper, Zoehrer, also hobbling, present Australia with a problem for the final match.

Australia failed to win because with some shoddy fielding, and another crass run-out preceding Waugh's, they were unable to take advantage of England's performance which, with one exception, was some way down on the slick effort at Old Trafford.

The exception was Allan Lamb, who completed his fourth one-day hundred for England from the last ball of the innings. It is hard in the circumstances to give him the low post-benefit profile he apparently craves, so he'll forgive me

Scoreboard from Trent Bridge

England won toss

England

		6s	4s	Mins	Balls
G A Gooch c Jones b Alderman	10	–	–	45	35
*D I Gower b Waugh	28	–	3	88	59
M W Gatting b May	37	–	3	104	76
A J Lamb not out	100	–	9	140	104
R A Smith st Healy b May	3	–	–	6	9
I T Botham run out (Border–May)	8	–	–	17	16
D R Pringle not out	25	–	2	51	32
Extras (lb 14, w 1)	15				
Total (5 wkts, 55 overs)	**226**				

†S J Rhodes, P A J DeFreitas, J E Emburey and N A Foster did not bat.

FALL OF WICKETS: 1–30, 2–57, 3–119, 4–123, 5–138.

BOWLING: Alderman 9–2–38–1 (nb 1); Lawson 11–0–47–0; Rackemann 11–1–37–0 (w 1); Waugh 11–1–47–1; May 11–1–35–2; Moody 2–0–8–0.

Australia

		6s	4s	Mins	Balls
D C Boon b Botham	28	–	2	77	39
G R Marsh lbw b Emburey	34	–	3	91	83
D M Jones b Emburey	29	–	3	52	47
A R Border c Rhodes b Pringle	39	–	3	65	58
S R Waugh run out (Gooch–Rhodes–Foster)	43	–	5	79	61
T M Moody run out (Gower–Rhodes)	10	1	–	12	7
†I A Healey not out	26	–	–	50	28
G F Lawson c Gooch b Foster	1	–	–	12	5
T B A May b DeFreitas	2	–	–	8	3
C G Rackeman not out	0	–	–	1	1
Extras (b 1, lb 6, w 7)	14				
Total (8 wkts, 55 overs)	**226**				

T M Alderman did not bat.

FALL OF WICKETS: 1–59, 2–81, 3–116, 4–153, 5–174, 6–205, 7–218, 8–225.

BOWLING: Foster 11–2–44–1 (w 2); DeFreitas 11–0–48–1 (nb 2, w 2); Pringle 11–1–38–1 (w 1); Botham 11–0–42–1 (w 2); Emburey 11–0–47–2.

Man of the Match: A J Lamb.

Umpires: H D Bird and J H Hampshire.

if I say that it was a brilliant effort, on a slow pitch where no other batsman was able adequately to adjust his timing, and typical of the genre: scoreboard ticking with singles and twos for the first part – just the one boundary in his first 45 runs – but then when the time is right, a stream of them, nine in all. His fifty took 71

ABOVE Gower explains the rules to Dean Jones as the Australian is ordered off the pitch by the umpires in the 'runner' controversy at Trent Bridge

BELOW England's keeper Steve Rhodes runs out Moody – Australia's nerves got the better of them as they chased England's total

balls, his hundred only 33 more. There was never another candidate for Man of the Match: the £350 he won, incidentally, is taxable.

Third Texaco Trophy One-Day International

England v Australia
Lord's, 29 May 1989

England 278–7
Australia 279–4
Australia won by 6 wickets

Australia won a momentous victory at Lord's when they beat England in the third one-day international by 6 wickets with three balls of the game remaining. That England take the series by virtue of having lost fewer wickets in Saturday's tie at Trent Bridge is immaterial: in the minds of everyone but those who drew up the competition rules it has been halved, with one win each and that tie. We all know one-day cricket is no barometer for the real thing, but the Ashes series could be a cracker.

It was a win that at one time had seemed way beyond reach for Australia. England, winning the toss and batting for the third time in a row, made 278 for 7 thanks to a brilliant innings of 136 from Graham Gooch and 61 from David Gower, with whom Gooch shared an opening stand of 123.

England must have been confident. But Geoff Marsh matched Gooch with a century of equal, if more placid, professionalism, and it proved to be the fulcrum for a remarkable win. When Tom Moody clipped Derek Pringle through mid-wicket for the winning run, Marsh had 111 to his name: he walked off to a standing ovation and, I could swear, the name 'Graham' attributed

to him by the public address system. Graham, one suspects, would not have been too delighted with 111; Geoff can be proud. With five overs of the game remaining, Australia had played themselves into the position where they needed 45. Most importantly, however, there were wickets in hand. Marsh was already approaching his century and, together with Steve Waugh, was picking up the pace. Marsh reached his seventh century in one-day internationals with an inside edge for four: nine came from DeFreitas's over.

The next over perhaps settled the issue. Waugh, a magnificently clean striker of the ball, twice in succession swung Foster, straying towards leg stump, high over mid-wicket for six. Suddenly, from nine an over, the rate was down to seven, and the wickets still in hand. Eight from Pringle's next over took it further down to just over a run a ball. Waugh promptly holed out mightily to Gooch at long on, but his 35 from 32 balls had relieved the pressure. Marsh then stroked Foster's last ball immaculately through mid-wicket for four, and the result was settled. Moody finished things off. Marsh was named as Man of the Match – as the adjudicator was Peter May, whose track record in such things is not good, it's a wonder it didn't go to Allan Lamb for his first-ball nought.

England, one feels, misread the crusty pitch, which began with moisture in it – goodness knows how on this sparkling blue Bank Holiday – and steadily improved throughout the day until by the end it was a belter. But at the start, against some disciplined Australian bowling, particularly from Alderman, both Gooch and Gower struggled to find their timing. They were canny enough, though, to keep the scoreboard clicking round with placement, and given the difficult circumstances the opening stand, from 31 overs, provided an unexpected platform. Gooch was able to add 57 more with Gatting and a similar number with Smith, before a final charge led by Botham, including a monsterously high six over long on, saw England to their total.

In the process, a single to square leg from his 135th ball had given Gooch his seventh one-day century for England with not a single blemish save the fortunate survival, when he had made

Scoreboard from Lord's

England won toss

England

	6s	4s	Mins	Balls
G A Gooch b Alderman	136	–	11	229	162
*D I Gower c Veletta b Moody.......	61	–	6	127	100
M W Gatting run out (Border–Alderman)	18	–	2	46	31
A J Lamb lbw Alderman	0	–	–	3	1
R A Smith b Rackemann................	21	–	1	37	22
I T Botham not out	25	1	3	21	11
P A J DeFreitas c Rackemann b Alderman	0	–	–	2	2
D R Pringle run out (Veletta–Waugh)	0	–	–	2	1
†S J Rhodes not out.......................	1	–	–	3	1
Extras (lb 14, w 2)......................	16				
Total (7 wkts, 55 overs)_____	**278**				

J E Emburey and N A Foster did not bat.
FALL OF WICKETS: 1–123, 2–180, 3–182, 4–239, 5–266, 6–266, 7–268.
BOWLING: Alderman 11–2–36–3 (w 1); Rackemann 11–0–56–1; Lawson 11–0–48–0 (w 1); Waugh 11–0–70–0; May 6–0–33–0 (nb 1); Moody 5–0–21–1.

Australia

	6s	4s	Mins	Balls
G R Marsh not out..........................	111	1	7	217	162
D C Boon lbw b Foster..................	19	–	3	21	17
D M Jones c Gower b Emburey......	27	–	2	71	67
*A R Border b Pringle....................	53	–	5	70	46
S R Waugh c Gooch b Foster.........	35	2	–	41	32
T M Moody not out	6	–	–	6	4
Extras (lb 18, w 9, nb 1)..............	28				
Total (4 wkts, 54.3 overs)_____	**279**				

†M R J Veletta, T B A May, G F Lawson, C G Rackemann and T M Alderman did not bat.
FALL OF WICKETS: 1–24, 2–84, 3–197, 4–268.
BOWLING: DeFreitas 11–1–50–0 (w 1); Foster 11–0–57–2 (w 1); Botham 11–0–43–0 (w 4); Pringle 10.3–0–50–1 (w 1, nb 1); Emburey 11–0–61–1 (w 2).

Man of the Match: G R Marsh.

Men of the Series: S R Waugh (Australia) and G A Gooch (England).

Umpires: B J Meyer and D R Shepherd.

37, of what appeared to be a legitimate run-out appeal, Boon hitting the bowler's stumps direct as Gooch tried to steal a single to mid-wicket. There were six fours in his hundred. Later, improvising marvellously, he hit a further five, before, with just nine balls of the innings remain-ing, Alderman sneaked a yorker under his bat as he made room to the leg side.

It was immediately evident at the start of the Australian innings that the pitch had improved. Now there was pace on the ball for the batsmen to be able to work the ball around the field. Boon drove DeFreitas emphatically through extra cover for four, but then fell lbw to Foster as he hit across a ball that pitched on middle-and-off and would have hit middle. Marsh and Dean Jones then took the score on to 84 with a 60-run second-wicket stand, before immediately after tea, Jones advanced down the pitch to Emburey and chipped gently to Gower at mid-wicket.

Now came the decisive innings. There is no one in the world more experienced in these matches than Allan Border, whose 187th match this was, and with Marsh chopping the seamers relentlessly down to third man, Border angling his runs off an open face, and both sweeping Emburey to distraction, the pair added 113 runs in 17 overs. Border had declared his intent by driving his first ball from Emburey through extra cover for four and it set him on the road to a half-century from 46 balls. Pringle, his erstwhile Essex colleague, bowled him with one that kept a little low as he shaped to pull, but by then the glimmer of a win was in the air. Marsh and Waugh saw it to fulfilment.

Postscript

Nobody surely, least of all the two sides concerned, can have been fooled into thinking that an Orwellian piece of rule-making, decreeing that although to all intents and purposes the sides finished the competition equal, England were more equal than Australia, gave David Gower anything other than the right to stand on the Lord's balcony and raise the trophy as high as his injured shoulder would allow.

The sides tied the series, of course they did, but if anyone had the right to be more equal than the other it was probably Australia, who recovered from an embarrassing, jittery start at

A century for Marsh and an Australian victory at Lord's in the third one-day international

ABOVE Botham hits out at Lord's – a shattered cheekbone would soon persuade him to wear a helmet

BELOW Moody leaps in vain as a massive hit from Botham goes for six

Old Trafford, would have won the tied match at Trent Bridge if their normally-brilliant running between the wickets hadn't let them down, and then triumphed magnificently at Lord's. Australia quite simply improved visibly as a team over the course of the three matches, gaining in confidence which will set them in good store for the Test matches. England, by contrast, peaked as a team in the first game when just about everything that David Gower touched turned to gold, and didn't aspire to such lofty heights again. After the first match, they leaned heavily on individual performances with the bat – Lamb at Trent Bridge, Gooch at Lord's – and the bowling never touched the professional, disciplined levels of Manchester

The series will probably be remembered, as one-day series tend to be, for deeds with the bat rather than parsimony with the ball. There could not have been a better sight than Gower royally marking his return as captain in the brief cameo which began hostilities. In the interest of team balance, Gower had decided to open the batting – although one hopes it's not a portent for the Test series – providing a wistful counterpoint to Gooch's brilliantly lugubrious and consistent play which brought him scores of 52, 10, and that exhilarating 136, and this partnership three times provided a solid base to the England innings.

At Nottingham, it was Lamb's turn to shine, with another marvellous century. He hates being saddled with the label of a one-day player, but it's really down to him. He has made a science of it, able to pace an innings to perfection, retaining his self-control where others might panic, stealing singles until he deems the moment right for the assault and then peppering the boundary. It was quite probably the innings of the series, although Gooch and Marsh will have run him close.

Although it is unwise to over-emphasise the significance of the series, it would not be unrealistic to suggest that the marked Australian improvement over the three matches, and the presence in particular of a group of technically well-schooled, orthodox batsmen could lead to a much more even, competitive Ashes series than many thought might be the case.

One-Day International Averages

England – batting and fielding

	M	I	NO	Runs	HS	100	50	Avge	Ct/St
A J Lamb	3	3	1	135	100*	1	–	67.50	–
G A Gooch........	3	3	0	198	136	1	1	66.00	2
D I Gower........	3	3	0	125	61	–	1	41.66	1
R A Smith	3	3	0	59	35	–	–	19.66	1
M W Gatting.....	3	3	0	58	37	–	–	19.33	–
I T Botham.......	3	3	1	37	25*	–	–	18.50	–
D R Pringle	3	3	1	34	25*	–	–	17.00	–
P A J DeFreitas.	3	2	1	17	17*	–	–	17.00	1
J E Emburey.....	3	1	0	10	10	–	–	10.00	1
S J Rhodes........	3	2	1	9	8	–	–	9.00	3
N A Foster	3	1	1	5	5*	–	–	–	–

Bowling

	O	M	R	W	BB	4w	Avge	R/O
N A Foster	32.0	5	130	6	3–29	–	21.66	4.06
J E Emburey......	33.0	0	139	6	3–31	–	23.16	4.21
D R Pringle	29.3	3	107	3	11–15	–	35.66	3.62
P A J DeFreitas.	30.0	4	118	3	2–19	–	39.33	3.93
I T Botham........	32.1	1	113	2	1–28	–	56.50	3.51

Australia – batting and fielding

	M	I	NO	Runs	HS	100	50	Avge	Ct/St
G R Marsh........	3	3	1	162	111*	1	–	81.00	–
S R Waugh........	3	3	0	113	43	–	–	37.66	–
I A Healy..........	2	2	1	36	26*	–	–	36.00	1/1
A R Border........	3	3	0	96	53	–	1	32.00	–
T M Moody.......	3	3	1	40	24	–	–	20.00	–
D M Jones........	3	3	0	60	29*	–	–	20.00	2
D C Boon........	3	3	0	52	28	–	–	17.33	2
M R J Veletta....	2	1	0	17	17	–	–	17.00	1
C G Rackemann	3	2	1	6	6	–	–	6.00	1
T B A May.......	2	1	0	2	2	–	–	2.00	–
G F Lawson	3	2	0	1	1	–	–	0.50	–
T M Alderman...	3	1	1	0	0*	–	–	–	1

Bowling

	O	M	R	W	BB	4w	Avge	R/O
T M Alderman ..	31.0	6	112	5	3–36	–	22.40	3.61
T B A May........	17.0	1	68	2	2–35	–	34.00	4.00
C G Rackemann	32.0	2	126	3	2–33	–	42.40	3.93
G F Lawson	33.0	1	143	3	3–48	–	47.66	4.33
S R Waugh........	33.0	2	162	3	2–45	–	54.00	4.90

ALSO BOWLED: A R Border 4–0–18–1; T M Moody 15–0–66–1.

Marsh and Boon could provide a formidable opening partnership, although until Marsh's wonderfully well-paced century at Lord's neither had exhibited the sort of unstoppable form shown in the warm-up games. There is the suggestion that for the Tests, Australia are keen to employ the left-handed Mark Taylor with Marsh as a variation, and drop Boon down the order. But the revelation of the Australian side must have been Steve Waugh, who was consistently able to come in when quick runs were needed and without resorting to anything other than pure strokes, provide them; witness the sixes he struck off Foster over the Tavern boundary to take the pressure off Australia in the final match.

It now remains to be seen whether England's selectors remain true to their declared intention of selecting a Test side without recourse to one-day cricket for reference. It is the bowlers and wicket-keeper to whom this may apply. De-Freitas, for example, is a pretty good one-day bowler, but his persistent movement into, rather than away from the bat, which is so restrictive to batsmen attempting to score quickly, is a disadvantage when trying to dismiss the same players on Test pitches. And can Botham's bowling now be regarded as a sufficient threat to justify his inclusion as an all-rounder? If not, does his batting merit his inclusion on its own? England will want to get things right for Headingley, where results are the norm, and Australian hearts tend to flutter. Get it wrong and the penalties could be severe.

PART TWO

First Cornhill Test Match

England v Australia, Headingley, 8–13 June 1989

Match Preview

It's hard to believe they have a cricket ground on Elm Street, but if they did, you can bet your life that in Aussie terms, it would look like Headingley. It has indeed been a nightmare for them. One has to drift back to 1964 for the last Australian victory on this ground when, with a nice sense of historical symmetry, the captains were Ted Dexter and Bobby Simpson, now England chairman and Aussie coach respectively.

Since then the picture has not been too pretty. A draw in 1968, followed in 1972 by a 9-wicket towelling thanks to a deadly combination of fuserium and Derek Underwood. Three years later, the George Davis dig-for-victory campaign sabotaged the pitch and ensured that Australia reached their zenith with a draw, since when it's been downhill – defeat by an innings and 42 in '77, followed by the biggest 500–1 horror of all in 1981, by 18 runs. Finally, when they were last here in 1985, under Allan Border, it was a 5-wicket loss. If England were looking for a psychological edge before the first salvo was let off then they couldn't have done better than to give Leeds the first Test.

It has, however, backfired slightly. England, remember, have been beaten in five of their last six Tests here and although the 'nightmare' may remain for Australia, England lost their Freddie Kruger when Ian Botham (whose reactions at slip, if not his fingers, are razor sharp) had his cheekbone eggshelled earlier in the week. The Australian reaction has been curious. Delight and double tinnies that he won't be there? Not on your Ned Kelly. 'We'd rather beat England with him in the side than in his hospital bed,' said Border yesterday. 'You can bet that if we do win, he'll say that we'd never have done it if he'd been there.' Australia, you could say, are determined to lay the ghost, which in the interests of a quiet summer would be a welcome change from barmaids.

In fact, the best intentions of both sides have plummeted this week. Mike Gatting tested his injured left thumb out during 25 minutes' practice yesterday afternoon, surviving in the process a beamer from an over-enthusiastic young net bowler, which he gloved over the back of the net. He emerged with a prognosis of 'fair', which like weather forecasts, could be taken optimistically or otherwise as you choose. Wisely though, no final decision will be taken until the morning of the match.

Australia suffered a potentially more damaging blow when Carl Rackemann, the man whom Border regards as his main strike bowler, was forced to withdraw with a knee injury that will require keyhole surgery. Rackemann has had his share of aches and pains over the years –

'I am not injury-prone,' he is known to argue semantically, 'just injury-plagued' – but he has looked the sharpest of the triumvirate he forms with Terry Alderman and Geoff Lawson. Four seamers, including the all-rounder Steve Waugh is a possibility now for them, with Merv the Moustache or Greg Campbell replacing Rackemann, and Tom Moody batting at number seven. David Gower predictably expresses thoughts of one-upmanship, as does Border, but realistically, both captains would probably be happy to survive unscathed with a draw.

But if anyone slept uneasily in his bed the night before the Test match it would surely have been the Headingley groundsman Keith Boyce. The teams can escape the nightmare; he has to live with it. However hard he tries, something always seems to happen here – last year, for instance, the drains burst beneath the run-ups – and there is no legislating for the Headingley micro-climate which can change Jekyll into Hyde before, as Arthur Askey used to say, your very eyes. This year's Test wicket was relaid three years ago and as such is the first over which he has had total control. It looks harmless enough, – no, better than that – but then they always do. Although there is nothing wrong with a result, eight in a row might seem excessive and Boyce more than anyone must be hoping for a draw.

First Test, 1st Day

Australia 207–3

Ah, the memories. It was at Headingley two years ago that Mike Gatting, captaining England against Pakistan, won the toss on a dingy morning, batted and saw his innings disintegrate in the first hour to 30-odd for 5. It earned him his Captain Cock-up soubriquet. Yesterday David Gower, in his first Test back in charge, and on the opening day of the Ashes series, did what Gatting might have done, winning the toss, glancing at sky, pitch, and Michael Fish's swirl-

ing weather charts and opting instead to field first.

But instead of England's four-pronged seam attack bringing the Australian dog smartly to heel, Gower first saw Geoff Marsh and Mark Taylor bat unscathed through a morning session shorn, through rain and bad light, of 10 overs, and then just when a measure of control seemed to have returned, with Marsh, in post-prandial stupor, lbw to the first ball of the afternoon and David Boon nicking fatally eight overs later, he could only watch helplessly as Taylor and Allan Border, the captain afloat on a sea of adrenalin, added 117 for the 3rd wicket in two hours and 20 minutes.

Although Border finally became a victim of his own aggression, top-edging DeFreitas's despairing bouncer to mid-wicket for 66, having hit nine fours, a six and a five, England were to gain no more success as Taylor and Dean Jones, who took five overs to get off the mark, saw out the day, by which time Australia had reached 207 for 3. Taylor, in only his fifth Test innings was within four runs of a maiden Test century at the close of play, and to compound Gower's day, was missed only once, by the England captain himself, a straightforward chance to third slip off Neil Foster with just three overs of the day remaining. Strange things happen on this ground, but Australia have already taken a firm hold on the match, and although there are miles to go, the tabloid knives were already glinting in the evening sunlight.

Curiously, an insertion that goes wrong always appears to be more heinous than the other option. Clearly, although the end could yet still justify the means, Gower, in his attempt to seize the early initiative with his seam attack, made an error of judgement, reading moisture into the pitch where there was none, and over-reacting to the cloud cover. In fact, and who can with absolute certainty predict such things, the pitch proved a toothless imitation of the horror it has been in the past: slow, and lacking bounce, which incidentally could prove the biggest problem later on. Keith Boyce the groundsman was naturally relieved – for 'reasonably happy' read 'yabadabadoo ...'. Just once has the pitch been used since it was relaid three years ago and that match, last August, produced 1285 runs for 18 wickets. Boyce knew what to expect. 'It is,' he said, 'like a young wine, still immature perhaps, but at least reliable.' Perhaps Gower, a wine buff, anticipated Hirondelle rather than Chateau Lafitte.

It was doubly embarrassing for England because they had opted to omit their only spinner, John Emburey, backing instead Phil DeFreitas (Gatting, by the way, failed his fitness test and Kim Barnett took his place). It was a partial success in that DeFreitas took two of the three wickets to fall, including Border, the other going to Foster, but when things go wrong an all-seam attack provides precious few options. It may prove no less of a problem later for Australia, who are similarly unbalanced. Emburey meanwhile has problems of his own. He is presently under a year's driving ban and has only a sponsored bike to get him to Middlesex's next game at Abergavenny; unless he tags on to the Milk Race, he might not make Saturday's start.

The day though, if not Gower's and England's, and in any case very much one of skirmishing, belonged to Taylor and Border. To accommodate Taylor, and his slip-catching, Australia have split the prolific Marsh–Boon opening partnership and although he lacks the aggression of Boon which so well complements Marsh's accumulative nature, it worked well yesterday. Left-handed, he was, until his let-off late in the day, always diligent outside the off-stump where in previous county matches he had seemed vulnerable, and drove pleasantly through the off-side at times, most notably when Newport, searching desperately for swing, overpitched.

But Taylor needed Border's company to provide stimulus to the innings. This match, indeed the series, is everything to the Australian captain who twice has been humiliated here. It showed. He may look like a small animal fresh out of hibernation when he blinks his way to the crease, but once there he just wrenched control from Gower, scything DeFreitas immediately over third man with a bat like a helicopter blade, and following it up next ball with an immaculate cover drive.

It set the tone as he then threw the bat wholeheartedly at anything within range, scoring as

Scoreboard from Headingley

England won toss

Australia

First Innings

	6s	4s	Mins	Balls
G R Marsh lbw b DeFreitas	16	–	1	80	63
M A Taylor not out	96	–	9	319	246
D C Boon c Russell b Foster	9	–	1	28	24
*A R Border c Foster b DeFreitas	66	1	9	140	118
D M Jones not out	10	–	1	66	41
Extras (lb 6, nb 4)	10				
Total (3 wkts, 81 overs)	**207**				

S R Waugh, †I A Healy, G D Campbell, M G Hughes, G F Lawson and T M Alderman to bat.
FALL OF WICKETS: 1–44, 2–57, 3–174.
BOWLING: DeFreitas 22–5–62–2 (nb 1); Foster 24–9–43–1; Newport 19–4–54–0 (nb 4); Pringle 14–2–36–0 (nb 1); Gooch 2–0–6–0.

England

G A Gooch, B C Broad, *D I Gower, A J Lamb, R A Smith, K J Barnett, †R C Russell, P J Newport, D R Pringle, P A J DeFreitas and N A Foster.

Umpires: D R Shepherd and J W Holder.

● A R Border's innings includes a five.

freely at times off edges as off the middle. One skimming, bat-hurling edge off DeFreitas took his total number of runs, in five fewer Tests, past Viv Richards's 7849. It puts him fourth in the pecking order, behind only Gavaskar, Boycott and Sobers, the latter two of whom he could also pass this series. When you consider how many of those runs have been battled out in adversity, it is a true measure of his worth.

First Test, 2nd Day

Australia 580–6

The ghost, it seems, has been exorcised. England took a caning from Australia today, the like of which they have not received on this ground since distant sepia pre-war, pre-Waugh days.

On a warm and mostly overcast day, the sages

had nodded wisely and suggested the ball might perform acrobatics. Instead, Australia – 207 for 3 overnight – scored 120 in the morning session, another 114 in the afternoon, and then, with the English bowling and fielding wilting, a further 139 after tea; 373 runs in the day. That is heady stuff and for England just three wickets to show for it, one in the first session and two in the second, as Australia reached the lofty heights of 580 for 6 – just four short of the highest made in a Test on this ground.

There was the foundation stone of a maiden Test century from Mark Taylor – who, 96 not out overnight, completed the job early in the day by glancing Pringle delicately to fine leg for four – and 79 quality runs from the precocious, cocksure bat of Dean Jones. There was even a half-century clubbed delightedly by Merv Hughes, which really is rubbing salt into the wounds. Overshadowing all of this, however, was an utterly glorious maiden Test century from Steve Waugh, whose unbeaten 174 was compiled in less than five hours, and contained some 24 boundaries and not a sniff of a chance.

Not one of England's four main bowlers escaped – Neil Foster, the pick by some way, Phil DeFreitas, Phil Newport and Derek Pringle let no one down with their effort, but none on the day were sufficiently persistent in the demands they made on the batsmen, with all conceding in excess of 100 runs.

Newport in fact topped the 150 but he did at least have the consolation of the wickets of Jones – suddenly confronted by the swing, seam and, crucially, bounce of an unplayable ball that had been conspicuously absent until then – and Healy, who chipped a simple return catch bang on tea.

The other wicket of the day was that of Taylor, who, after batting 6½ hours for 136 was lbw to Foster misjudging the length, and pulling fatally.

Century partnerships were the norm too: the 138 that Jones and Waugh plundered in 31 overs won't be bettered this summer for quality, while the biggest of the innings, 139 in 32 between Waugh and Hughes, was grand entertainment. Taylor and Jones managed a mere doctor's orders.

Waugh is only just 24 and this was his first hundred, but he is an experienced Test cricketer – this was his 42nd innings in 27 Tests. Although he twice reached the nineties against West Indies, he had never progressed beyond. The maiden hundred which in the past had proved equally elusive for such subsequently heavy-scorers as Mike Gatting and Bobby Simpson, was indeed a while coming. But his talent, as anyone who watched Somerset last summer will testify, was never doubted. His batting, demeanour and even appearance evoke Corinthian memories of old. He is slight of build, pale and slim as a celery stick, with chiselled, angular cigarette-card features beneath the baggy green cap he favours rather than a helmet.

He is not classically elegant in the manner of, say, Greg Chappell, nor brutal like Richards. And he is perhaps too explosive, particularly off the back foot, to be called dapper. Back in 1930 and '34 on this ground, when bowlers were ritually sacrificed on Bradman's altar as he creamed out triple hundreds and Australia made 566 and 584 respectively, Stan McCabe made 27 and 30, and those who remember (and there were a few at Leeds yesterday) say that it is him that Waugh resembles uncannily at the crease. That is praise indeed, for McCabe's 232 at Nottingham in 1938 is credited with being one of the greatest ever, astounding even the Don.

Yesterday, Waugh was uncomplicated, making certain on this pitch, with its occasional low bounce, that he got well forward. His driving on both sides of the wicket was clipped as precisely as a colonel's moustache and when the bowlers inevitably dropped shorter, he flailed away outside off-stump, cutting them to ribbons. Later, it was only Barnett's enthusiasm on the extra-cover boundary which remotely blocked the flow.

And when there was no boundary to hit, he was able, as was Jones – whose innings, incidentally, was overshadowed but in no way demeaned by Waugh – to taunt England's cumbersome fielders with singles pushed and shuttled with stunning confidence and simplicity, like picking pockets. The running of these two was of the highest class and ran England ragged.

It was an hour and a quarter before Waugh joined Jones at the crease, by which time the new

LEFT The turning point of the series as Gower wins the toss at Headingley and puts Australia in

BELOW Steve Waugh took full advantage and notched his first ever Test hundred

ABOVE Fighting back for England – Lamb on his way to a spirited hundred at Headingley

RIGHT Australian slips (left to right) Taylor, Alderman and Border

Scoreboard from Headingley

Australia

First innings

		6s	4s	Mins	Balls
G R Marsh lbw b DeFreitas	16	–	1	80	63
M A Taylor lbw b Foster	136	–	16	392	315
D C Boon c Russell b Foster	9	–	1	28	24
*A R Border c Foster b Defreitas	66	1	9	140	118
D M Jones c Russell b Newport	79	–	7	265	172
S R Waugh not out	174	–	24	286	233
†I A Healy c and b Newport	16	–	2	37	31
M G Hughes not out	63	2	5	123	94
Extras (lb 13, w 1, nb 7)	21				
Total (6 wkts, 173 overs)	**580**				

G D Campbell, G F Lawson and T M Alderman to bat.
FALL OF WICKETS: 1–44, 2–57, 3–174, 4–273, 5–411, 6–441.
BOWLING: DeFreitas 43–7–128–2 (nb 1); Foster 43–13–100–2 (w 1); Newport 39–5–153–2 (nb 6); Pringle 33–5–123–0 (nb 4); Gooch 9–1–31–0; Barnett 6–0–33–0 (nb 1).

England

G A Gooch, B C Broad, *D I Gower, A J Lamb, R A Smith, K J Barnett, †R C Russell, P J Newport, D R Pringle, P A J DeFreitas and N A Foster.

ball had come and gone, and Jones, who had been batting for 35 overs, was already 34. 27 overs later, Waugh had 76 and had roared past him. His hundred, reached with yet another off-side smear to the deep sweeper, had taken 124 balls, with 16 fours. He saluted team mates and then crowd, knocked his chewing gum away and took fresh guard. The rest was inevitable. Great days.

First Test, 3rd Day

Australia 601–7 dec, England 284–4

When David Gower won the toss and decided to put Australia in, he made a decision which, should England lose, is destined to be labelled one of the biggest gaffes an England cricket captain has made. The gamble, as Gower freely admits, went wrong, but may well, by the close of the match, prove not as dramatically so as it seemed on Friday evening. Allan Border doesn't discount the possibility of a bold declaration but if, as seems likely, England score the remaining 114 they need to avoid following on, it will have just been one means of arriving at the same drawn end.

It would, in any case, have been a brave man who came out strongly against Gower's move at 11 o'clock on Thursday morning. Consider Gower's position. Rightly or wrongly, and based on a historical fact that spinners have in the past 10 years taken a mere tenth of the Test wickets that have fallen at Headingley, he and the selectors had opted to go into the match with an all-seam attack and while the facile argument is to suggest that if spinners don't bowl they can't take wickets, the plain truth is that because the seamers have been successful, even when the pitch has turned a spinner has been surplus to requirements.

Gower reasoned several things. Firstly, with his attack, they and he had a better chance of taking the early initiative by getting wickets on the first morning when the pitch would be at its most moist, surmising – correctly as it has turned out – that it would improve on the second and third days, by which time he would reasonably have hoped to have dismissed Australia and be well into his own innings. The decision was further based on the weather conditions at the time (overcast, if chilly) a prognosis of further bad weather which may have shortened the match, and a belief – 'instinct' he later called it – that it was the way to go. He was also understandably reluctant to take too much notice of the groundsman's advice that the pitch would be a belter, believing him to be crying wolf. 'Keith Boyce has been saying his pitches are belters for seven years,' said Gower on Saturday while conceding that 'perhaps we should give him a pat on the back this time.'

Having come to his conclusion however Gower at least had the right to expect that his bowlers would perform as Test players, and in this he was, with the exception of Neil Foster, woefully let down. Phil DeFreitas, Phil Newport and Derek Pringle were all guilty of failure to adhere to the basics when things were going badly, just when Gower wanted the sort of control that Hendrick, say, or Old used to give Mike Brearley. That, except for the fact that he was instrumental in their selection, and might well have been more imaginative in his captaincy (where Border has already outshone him), is not Gower's fault.

Yet balanced criticism, as opposed to instant hysteria, is only possible with the benefit of a huge dollop of hindsight. 'Of course it was wrong to put them in if they got 600', will be the view. But just because Border says he would have batted first doesn't mean his rationale was any better; he, remember, had no spinner either to utilise a wearing fifth-day pitch.

And what in any case if England were to go and get 600 themselves? The pitch, while by no means perfect, with occasional erratic bounce, has played well enough for the paucity of bowling on both sides to be witheringly exposed by a succession of batsmen in prime form, beginning with Taylor, Waugh, Border and Jones for Australia and then Barnett and Lamb in England's reply.

Both England players played superbly but what a contrast these two display at the crease. Kim Barnett still surely comes into the category of poor technicians who are destroyers of mediocre bowling on good pitches (or bad for that matter) but who would be sorely tested by a better attack than this. He fidgets and moves around like no Test player since Randall and commits himself early in so doing. His stroke-play on Saturday was jaunty and exhilarating, but the way in which he reached his half-century for example, a drive smashed at catchable height through square cover, is not the stuff of Test matches, and although he might have been unlucky with the lbw decision that removed him, its manner – hitting horribly around his front pad – is a telling factor.

Allan Lamb by contrast can and did look a complete batsman, a feature of which is his orthodox stance (how many of the very best players in the world have anything other than this?) and steadiness of head at the crease that Barnett lacks. He has wonderful controlling

Scoreboard from Headingley

Australia

First Innings

		6s	4s	Mins	Balls
G R Marsh lbw b DeFreitas	16	–	1	80	63
M A Taylor lbw b Foster	136	–	16	392	315
D C Boon c Russell b Foster	9	–	1	28	24
*A R Border c Foster b DeFreitas	66	1	9	140	118
D M Jones c Russell b Newport	79	–	7	265	172
S R Waugh not out	177	–	24	306	243
†I A Healy c and b Newport	16	–	2	37	31
M G Hughes c Russell b Foster	71	2	6	132	105
G F Lawson not out	10	–	1	11	13
Extras (lb 13, w 1, nb 7)	21				
Total (7 wkts dec, 178 overs)	**601**				

G D Campbell and T M Alderman did not bat.
FALL OF WICKETS: 1–44, 2–57, 3–174, 4–273, 5–411, 6–441, 7–588.
BOWLING: DeFreitas 45.3–8–140–2 (nb 2); Foster 46–14–109–3 (w 1); Newport 39–5–153–2 (nb 4); Pringle 33–5–123–0 (nb 1); Gooch 9–1–31–0; Barnett 6–0–32–0.

England

First Innings

		6s	4s	Mins	Balls
G A Gooch lbw b Alderman	13	–	2	58	46
B C Broad b Hughes	37	–	5	107	74
K J Barnett lbw b Alderman	80	–	10	164	118
A J Lamb not out	103	–	19	241	177
*D I Gower c Healy b Lawson	26	–	5	59	38
R A Smith not out	16	–	3	62	46
Extras (b 4, lb 1, nb 4)	9				
Total (4 wkts, 82 overs)	**284**				

D R Pringle, †R C Russell, P J Newport, P A J DeFreitas and N A Foster to bat.
FALL OF WICKETS: 1–35, 2–81, 3–195, 4–243.
BOWLING: Alderman 23–5–60–2 (nb 2); Lawson 22–4–74–1 (nb 1); Campbell 8–0–39–0 (nb 3); Border 2–1–5–0; Hughes 21–6–74–1; Waugh 6–2–27–0 (nb 1).

hands, too, and plays ramrod straight. Contrary to Gower's belief, few have ever doubted Lamb's ability to bat; merely his aptitude to consistently put it on display in Tests. On Saturday he paraded his talent in all its finery, dealing in boundaries – 19 in all – hooked ferociously and driven through the off-side particularly with absolute contempt. When he smashed Lawson through extra cover to reach his first hundred in 12 tests against Australia, he at least will have known that his place for the summer, marginal before this match, will have been secured.

First Test, 4th Day

Australia 601–7 dec, and 158–3
England 430

Twenty minutes after lunch today, Jack Russell, England's wicket keeper, leaned forward to a rare half-volley from Terry Alderman, and pushed it through the vacant mid-off area and down the Headingley hill to the football stand boundary for four. It took England's first innings total to 404 for 7, and so past the follow-on mark of 402. In so doing, it virtually condemned the match – barring the miracles which have of course been known to happen here – to a draw, although England may have an uneasy final day.

Beginning the day at 284 for 4, still needing 118 to avoid the follow-on, they lost both Allan Lamb, for 125, and Derek Pringle, cheaply, to the new ball, for the addition of 54. A seventh-wicket stand between Robin Smith (66) and Phil Newport (36) doubled that before Smith was out with just 10 wanted. Once that had been achieved, though not without a couple of hiccups, the England lower order collapsed to Alderman and Geoff Lawson, and they were all out for 430, having lost their last six wickets yesterday for 146, leaving a deficit of 171. Alderman's skilful persistence was rewarded with figures of 5 for 107.

Assuming they didn't subsequently play like nerds – a rash assumption – England were now, with only slightly more than four sessions left to play, theoretically out of the wood. But Allan Border had intimated on Saturday that he might consider a declaration in an attempt still to force a win, and if not, to at least make England sweat for a while.

First, though, his batsmen would have to score enough runs at a sufficient rate to put the match indisputably beyond England's reach – Border has suffered enough agonies at Headingley to risk any sort of gamble – while at the same time rendering the exercise worthwhile. In the event, thanks to another half-century from Mark Taylor to go with his first innings century, 43 from Boon, and a rumbustuous 31 from Border they reached 158 for 3 before a premature close with a lead of 329, which is already more than England have ever successfully chased in a home Ashes series.

There was a hint of controversy at the end of the day. With three overs remaining the umpires, David Shepherd and John Holder, took the players from the field because of bad light and a slight drizzle, a decision with which Border obviously disagreed: he stayed at the crease to remonstrate angrily as the covers were being put on. It was, admittedly, very gloomy, but he had a point, in view of the fact that he and Jones had just taken 28 runs from the previous two overs bowled by Foster and DeFreitas, neither a slouch in terms of pace. The light was incapacitating only to the fielding side, and the pitch at that point was not in immediate danger of a dowsing. Still it is the umpires who, in the event of a disagreement between the captains on whether play should continue (Gower obviously wanted to get off), are the sole arbiters of fitness for play. It was nonetheless a daft decision of the sort that are both incomprehensible to the public and bad PR but within the laws.

When Lamb and Smith resumed in the morning they knew that the new ball was due in three overs, and this would probably provide make-or-break for Australia. Lamb, keen to make the most of the old ball, with which Border persisted for eight overs, began the day by peppering the boundary.

At 320 for 4 came the crunch, and the eleventh delivery with the harder ball did for Lamb, who pushed forward to Alderman only for the ball to deviate in slightly, and bounce in a gentle parabola via pad and glove to Boon at short leg. His had been a high-class knock in any circumstances, and all the more commendable for the way he carried the attack to Australia. The

Scoreboard from Headingley

Australia

First innings: 601 for 7 dec (M A Taylor 136, A R Border 66, D M Jones 79, S R Waugh 177 not out, M G Hughes 71).

Second Innings

		6s	4s	Mins	Balls
M A Taylor c Broad b Pringle	60	–	8	121	112
G R Marsh c Russell b Foster	6	–	–	22	22
D C Boon lbw b DeFreitas	43	–	6	138	95
*A R Border not out	31	–	6	53	38
D M Jones not out	12	–	1	12	8
Extras (lb 1, w 1, nb 4)	6				
Total (3 wkts, 45 overs)	**158**				

S R Waugh, †I A Healy, G F Lawson, G D Campbell, M G Hughes and T M Alderman to bat.

FALL OF WICKETS: 1–14, 2–97, 3–129.
BOWLING: Foster 16–4–49–1 (w 1); DeFreitas 15–2–54–1 (nb 3); Pringle 9–1–32–1 (nb 2); Newport 5–2–22–0 .

England

First Innings

		6s	4s	Mins	Balls
G A Gooch lbw b Alderman	13	–	2	58	46
B C Broad b Hughes	37	–	5	107	74
K J Barnett lbw b Alderman	80	–	10	164	118
A J Lamb c Boon b Alderman	125	–	24	279	205
*D I Gower c Healy b Lawson	26	–	5	59	38
R A Smith lbw b Alderman	66	–	8	189	132
D R Pringle lbw b Campbell	6	–	1	14	15
P J Newport c Boon b Lawson	36	–	3	142	73
†R C Russell c Marsh b Lawson	15	–	3	52	33
P A J DeFreitas lbw b Alderman	1	–	–	9	6
N A Foster not out	2	–	–	5	5
Extras (b 5, lb 7, w 1; nb 10)	23				
Total (121.5 overs)	**430**				

FALL OF WICKETS: 1–35, 2–81, 3–195, 4–243, 5–323, 6–338, 7–392, 8–421, 9–424.
BOWLING: Alderman 37–7–107–5 (nb 4); Lawson 34.5–6–105–3 (w 1, nb 1); Campbell 14–0–82–1 (nb 8); Border 2–1–5–0; Hughes 28–7–92–1; Waugh 6–2–27–0 (nb 1).

24 fours he hit were an extraordinarily high percentage of runs in innings of that length. When Pringle was lbw to Campbell – unluckily as it appeared – giving the bowler his first Test wicket and some consolation for a chastening debut, England were still in trouble. Smith and Newport however showed belligerence when it was most

needed, with Smith batting for over three hours for his 66 before becoming the sixth lbw victim out of 13 wickets that had fallen thus far. Alderman and Lawson polished things off.

Alderman's effort was just reward for showing the basic qualities that had been lacking in all the other bowlers in the match except for Foster and, at times, Hughes. He has lost a couple of yards of pace and nip since the terrible shoulder dislocation he suffered in Perth seven years ago while attempting a citizen's arrest on a pitch invader, and it clearly takes several overs for his joint to loosen. But he is a shrewd, guileful operator now bowling from close to the stumps so that the ball travels in a line from wicket to wicket. 'Lbw Alderman' is now a frequent scoresheet entry, and done in the classical manner with away swing that, unlike the dreaded nip-backer, brooks no argument.

First Test, 5th Day

Australia 601–7 dec, and 230–3 dec
England 430, and 191
Australia won by 210 runs

The brave new world of English cricket was looking decidedly tawdry all of a sudden as the sound of rock music and popping champagne corks eminated from the Australian dressing room. If a single Australian raises his head from the pillow on Wednesday morning without the feeling that someone is trying to pickaxe his way out, then he must be a fifth columnist, for they had every reason to celebrate. There were still almost 28 overs of the match remaining when Merv Hughes, trundling down the hill from the Kirkstall Lane like a runaway freight train, knocked back Phil DeFreitas's middle stump. Pandemonium broke out. In 55 overs, on a pitch that had until the start of England's second innings yielded 1261 runs at a cost of 20 wickets, the Australian seamers had raised their game when it was most needed and bowled England

ABOVE The two captains stroll wearily off as the match seemingly heads for a draw

BELOW Gooch is trapped lbw by Hughes and the scoreboard shows England's predicament on the final day

A confident appeal from Hughes ...

... and Australia have clinched victory in the First Test match

Ted Dexter looks concerned – but not concerned enough to be at Headingley on the final day, according to some Press critics

out for 191, giving Australia victory in the first Test by 210 runs.

The principal soloist in what was a well-orchestrated piece from Allan Border – whose subsequent champagne-soaked joy it was hard, even for Englishmen, not to share – was Terry Alderman who gave a masterly exhibition of fast-medium bowling to take 5 for 44 which, with his five wickets in the first innings, gave him outstanding match figures of 10 for 151.

England therefore have won just one of their last 20 Tests – Sri Lanka last summer – since beating Australia in Melbourne almost three years ago. And their own version of what is popularly known as the 'Headingley Hoodoo' continues, having lost six of the last seven Tests played on this ground; at least one to all the Test playing nations except Sri Lanka, and that no doubt is only because they have yet to play in Leeds.

In terms of the series, it is not the end of the world. There are five more Tests to go and Gower has come from behind before to win a series. Remember, too, that Australia won the first Test of the 1981 Ashes series, before Dr Brearley, with a bit of help from Beefy, intervened. But Australian spirits are sky-high. To suggest that England were disappointing would be an understatement. They certainly went into the last day under pressure and nothing to do but survive. But that is the very essence of Test cricket and it is hard to remember when an England side last played with such a total lack of conviction against anyone other than West Indies. Only Graham Gooch, who batted phlegmatically and skilfully for close on three hours to make 68 showed the necessary degree of application to survive the best part of a day, once England had been set an impossible target of 402. Kim Barnett made 34 in his buffeting style, without remotely approaching Gooch's air of permanence. Ditto David Gower who also made 34, with six boundaries, but was suckered down the leg side for the second time in the match. No one else, until DeFreitas threw the bat at the end, reached double figures.

The critical part of the day came between lunch and tea. England had, by the first interval, reached 66 for the single loss of Chris Broad, lbw to a ball from Alderman that kept horribly low, and there was no reason to expect the sort of carnage that came. 'We thought the game might have slipped away at that point,' admitted Border later. Instead, England contrived to lose six wickets for 88 in the session and once more it was Alderman who led the charge. Barnett, who still hops about in the crease as if treading the vintage, seemed to be caught in two minds when Alderman dropped short, and edged the fifth ball of the afternoon low to Taylor at first slip.

Lamb, after one thunderous boundary, pushed forward too stiffly, bat well ahead of pad, and Boon, who makes a point of standing deeper than has been the fashion, was able to take a sharp catch at short square-leg that might have eluded a closer fielder.

Gooch and Gower then added 57, before it was Lawson's turn to intervene. Gower had already glanced a boundary gossamer-fine and Lawson immediately countered by posting a leg slip. Undeterred, Gower flicked outside leg-stump once more and Healy, moving sharply across to the leg side, took an important catch one-handed. Smith followed four balls later, caught at third slip.

The crucial wicket though, that of Gooch, went to Hughes, who, recalled by Border to the Kirkstall Lane End, saw his first ball disappear through square leg and the second win yet another lbw decision as Gooch perhaps shuffled too far across his stumps. It would be kindest to say nothing about Pringle's dismissal or his Test in general, but he may well not make Lord's. It removed the necessity for Border's bowlers to push too hard, and relaxed as they were, Hughes and Alderman finished the job.

Afterwards, Gower admitted that Australia had outplayed them in all departments, which is true only up to a point. Certainly they batted very well, with centuries from Taylor and Waugh matched in quality only by Lamb and yesterday, on a high, the lot of them caught everything that moved except the obligatory streaker.

But the crucial difference lay in the bowling. England were unable to exploit a pitch which although slow and, in Headingley terms, benign, still offered some help to the seamer who was

Australia

First innings: 601 for 7 dec (M A Taylor 136, A R Border 66, D M Jones 79, S R Waugh 177 not out, M G Hughes 71).

Second Innings

		6s	4s	Mins	Balls
M A Taylor c Broad b Pringle.........	60	–	8	121	112
G R Marsh c Russell b Foster..........	6	–	–	22	22
D C Boon lbw b DeFreitas	43	–	6	138	95
*A R Border not out	60	–	8	96	76
D M Jones not out	40	–	3	55	34
Extras (lb 2, lb 5, w 9, nb 5)........	21				
Total (3 wkts dec, 54.5 overs)	**230**				

S R Waugh, †I A Healy, G F Lawson, G D Campbell, M G Hughes and T M Alderman did not bat.

FALL OF WICKETS: 1–14, 2–97, 3–129.
BOWLING: Foster 19–4–65–1 (w 2); DeFreitas 18–2–76–1 (w 1, nb 3); Pringle 12.5–1–60–1 (nb 7); Newport 5–2–22–0.

England

First innings: 430 (K J Barnett 80, A J Lamb 125, R A Smith 66; T M Alderman 5 for 107).

Second Innings

		6s	4s	Mins	Balls
G A Gooch lbw b Hughes	68	–	10	175	118
B C Broad lbw b Alderman	7	–	1	18	12
K J Barnett c Taylor b Alderman....	34	–	7	51	46
A J Lamb c Boon b Alderman.........	4	–	1	8	6
*D I Gower c Healy b Lawson	34	–	6	51	44
R A Smith c Border b Lawson.........	0	–	–	5	3
D R Pringle c Border b Alderman..	0	–	–	38	27
P J Newport c Marsh b Alderman...	8	–	1	39	27
†R C Russell c Healy b Hughes.......	2	–	–	26	22
P A J DeFreitas b Hughes	21	–	3	25	18
N A Foster not out	1	–	–	18	16
Extras (b 4, lb 3, nb 5)................	12				
Total (55.2 overs)	**191**				

FALL OF WICKETS: 1–17, 2–67, 3–77, 4–134, 5–136, 6–153, 7–153, 8–166, 9–170.
BOWLING: Alderman 20–7–44–5 (nb 4); Lawson 11–2–58–2; Campbell 10–0–42–0 (nb 3); Hughes 9.2–2–36–3; Border 5–3–4–0.

Man of the match: T M Alderman.

prepared to give it a chance. Alderman used the conditions brilliantly, consistently forcing the batsmen to play, while England, particularly on the first day wavered too far and too often in line and length. It allowed the Australian batsmen the luxury of waiting for the bad ball secure in the knowledge that it would arrive sooner rather than later. It is already time for an England rethink. This was not just a question of the right players performing below par; mistakes were made in selection, a situation not helped by the injuries to Mike Gatting and Ian Botham. Gower will be hard pushed to stay loyal to the bowlers he helped select here and only Foster may survive.

Postscript

David Gower is not an outwardly emotional man, but he looked mighty close to tears as he sat in the players' dining room to face the press after what was one of the most humiliating defeats England have suffered in many years. 'Disappointed, David?' A stare at the array of microphones in front of him, then a gulp. 'Yup.' He may be in his thirties now, but there is still something essentially boyish about Gower's demeanour, and he carried the air of a lad who'd been caught scrumping.

Being captain of England carries its many benefits, as half the current side could testify. But they would also add that when things go wrong, it's a lonely hilltop they occupy. You take the plaudits for what is generally a team effort – and a lot of decisions made by captains are the result of corporate input – but in the past 20 Tests there haven't been many of those. Instead, cans have been carried. Gower was trying to come to terms with the decision to put Australia in which, it will be argued, cost England the match. It was, he had said earlier in the match, his instinct which had led him to the decision, but one suspects that that was just Gowerese for something which appeared the rational, logical thing to do at the time, and a decision at which he would not have arrived alone.

Life though can make a mockery of rational thought. The pitch was not unhelpful, as Border confirmed, and Gower had every reason to expect his bowlers to perform like internationals and gain what benefit there was; instead they bowled like tarts. It was their failure, not the toss of a coin, which cost England the match. Once

Australia had survived, with only three wickets down, a day they may well have faced with trepidation beforehand, the balance not only of power but of self-belief had shifted. 'It came down to that first day,' was Allan Border's assessment. 'Because of some of the problems we have had here, that was a very difficult day for us.' The marvellous century from Waugh was merely an inevitable consequence of the groundwork that Taylor in particular had laid with his own maiden Test century. If England, before the match, had anticipated Australian Headingley paranoia giving them a winning opportunity they would have been greatly disappointed. The best England could hope for, once Australia had made 600, was a draw.

'We are aware,' said Gower, composure recovered now, 'that over five days, we haven't all performed to our capabilities. They out-performed us in all departments.' One person outperformed the lot though, for while all England's batsmen made some sort of score during the match, nobody came close to matching the performance of Terry Alderman with the ball. There have been sceptics who have suggested that the Australian attack has the resilience of rice pudding skin, and certainly there have been moments on the tour when the creaks of Alderman's shoulder and Rackemann's knee, and the twanging protest of ageing hamstrings have been almost symphonic. Certainly Alderman takes time to warm up now, easing rather than heaving his shoulder joint into action. But once under way, he operates like no other bowler in the land, bowling relentlessly straight and wicket-to-wicket, with lbws his stock in trade. By contrast, English bowlers these days are increasingly flattered by a potent cocktail of bad pitches and a ball stitched with piano wire, which make masters out of mediocrity. So it comes as a shock to the system when more is required than simply to bowl-it-and-hope.

It would have come as no surprise to Gower the day after the game to have been greeted by tabloid derision. But Ted Dexter as well was subjected to a volley for not being, as they put it, on the bridge when the ship went down. Quite why it was thought he should have been there on the last day – he had seen the first three days and was in his office in London during the last-day debacle – when his brief doesn't demand it, is clear only to the sort of ten-bob-suit tabloid columnists who pen their comments apparently from their own back lawn. Dexter was appointed as chairman of the new England committee of which selection is only a part. And once the final team has been picked on the morning of the match, that, as far as he is concerned, is the limit of his involvement. He has, after all, a manager, Micky Stewart, in permanent attendance, and a managing director, Gower, on the field. Quite simply, Dexter believes in captaincy without interference. 'The players do not want selectors in the dressing room,' is his view.

Australia go to Lord's then with a unified team and the only unenforced change will surely be a spinner for Campbell, who is so green he is positively ozone-friendly. But where do England go from here? When Dexter took over from Peter May, it was his intention to back players chosen, giving them the security of a run of matches in which to prove themselves, rather than the swingeing changes in adversity that had become the norm. But changes, particularly to the bowling, have to be made. There is a worry too about Gower's participation. His long-standing shoulder injury had worsened during the Test to the extent that he was anticipating seeking specialist advice and possibly exploratory and manipulative treatment on the Friday following. He was keen to stress that he would in no way jeopardise his England place; Dexter took the pragmatic view that any one who seeks such treatment must by definition, irrespective of treatment, be doubtful. Ah well, England have had five captains in their last six Tests, so why not another. The wheel could go full circle of course: Mike Gatting has not played a Test since the debacle at Old Trafford last year. If he returns for Lord's, it could be as skipper.

Second Cornhill Test Match

England v Australia, Lord's, 22–27 June 1989

Match Preview

On Friday and Saturday, 22 and 23 June 1934, in the Second Test against Australia at Lord's, England made a creditable 440 in their first innings, and by close of play on the second day Australia had built a steady reply, reaching 192 for 2. Just before six o'clock on the Monday, around six playing hours later, the match was all over. Rain during the weekend – it happened in those days as well – had turned the pitch into a glutinous 'sticky dog', and Hedley Verity's left-arm spin had exploited this to perfection. He took 7 for 61 and 8 for 43: 15 for 104 in the match and 14 of them on that final day. England had won by an innings and 38 runs.

As England begin their attempt to repair the damage of Headingley, this delve into the mists of time is not without relevance, for Australia have enjoyed a love affair with Lord's that far exceeds any hate relationship that may have existed with Leeds, and that victory, 55 years ago was the last time St John's Wood witnessed an England victory in an Ashes Test. The trauma, in fact goes deeper: it is the only occasion this century it has happened, since when there have been eight draws and Australia have won five times.

Allan Border, dinkum bloke that he is, insists that past records count for nought when you line up for a fresh match, although he was keen enough to lay the ghost of Headingley. But on previous tours, never mind the actual outcome of the series concerned, Lord's has been a happy hunting ground for him. In 1981, as today, Australia came here having won the first Test, and Border made 64 and 12 not out in a drawn game. It was a watershed though, as the England captain, one I T Botham, bagged a pair, resigned the captaincy, and the rest, thanks to him and the old grey brainbox Brearley, is history. In 1985, Australia went one better, winning by four wickets a match in which Border, with innings of 196 and 41 not out, scored 43% of his side's runs. Both series Australia subsequently lost.

This Test, in spite of Australia's current crest and England's Phd – post-Headingley Depression – could be a close-run thing, depending, with the pitch promising to be as good as you can get here (if it's not, then questions will be asked), on the bowling and the response of key players to injury.

News of these, and the prospective eleven that England in particular will field, is hard to come by these days with no one wishing, as they put it, to give anything away to the enemy, which seems a bit puerile. But Allan Lamb had a fitness test on his injured finger, announced it easier than it was and will make a decision on the morning of the match; John Emburey's dislocated finger on his left hand is no problem now, Mike Gatting's thumb has healed; and David Gower's shoulder satisfies him, after its weekend manipulation. For Australia, Tim May is still out, possibly terminally, with a pulled hamstring and Carl Rackemann has yet to recover from his knee operation. The umpires have reported fit and well.

If England all similarly report on Thursday morning, then the implications are that Kim Barnett and Angus Fraser will be omitted from the England squad of thirteen. Despite Micky Stewart's observations that Fraser's local knowledge would be invaluable, Dexter has said that he is merely cover for Dilley: if Dilley plays then Fraser doesn't is the message. With Emburey sure to play, there is a case, in fact, for playing horses for courses, picking both Jarvis and Fraser and omitting instead Neil Foster, whose Lord's record – 8 wickets at 57 apiece from 6 Tests – is way below par; it is unlikely to happen, of course. About as likely in fact as Gatting failing to make his Test Match return, despite a record that has seen 183 runs at 16.6 from his last dozen innings, and 15 balls in first-class cricket since facing the Australians in the one-day international at Lord's a month ago.

Australia would also like to field a more balanced attack than at Headingley, but May's indisposition leaves only Trevor Hohn's leg spin, and while Border will be mindful that Bob Holland's wrist spin was instrumental in the last win here in 1985, he could well rely on himself to supply any relief from seam. The only Australian change, then, could be a batsman, Moody, for Greg Campbell, with Steve Waugh expected to bowl more. That extra batsman could ensure a draw.

Second Test, 1st Day

England 286, Australia 4–0

A cursory glance through conditions for Tests in this country shows no mention that the Law of Sod applies. After the first day's events at Lord's, David Gower may have cause to disagree.

Castigated at Headingley for watching Australia amass 600 having put them in to bat, he not only won the toss yesterday for the eighth time in as many flips with Allan Border, but with the clouds pressing overhead for the first time in ages, and fielding what he probably considers his best available seam attack, he would have been sorely tempted once again to put Australia in. He just couldn't though, could he? Instead, with a gulp no doubt, he opted, to ironic cheers from the crowd, to bat first, and of course the inevitable happened: England slumped, by midway through the afternoon, to 191 for 7, of which Graham Gooch made a stoical 60 and Gower a rather more fanciful 57. That they subsequently climbed to the dizzy heights of 286 before Terry Alderman finished off the innings as soon as the second new ball became available was entirely due to the efforts of the England keeper Jack Russell, who made an unbeaten 64 out of 101 scored while he was at the crease. It left the Australian openers to negotiate an unnerving single over from Graham Dilley, and this they successfully managed to do, reducing the deficit by four in the process.

This was no magical performance by the Australian seamers, who shared the wickets on as near perfect a pitch as you are likely to get at Lord's. The ball swung in the morning for Alderman, and seamed a little for the energetic, bustling Hughes and Lawson. But no more surely than might be expected on the first morning of a Test. The Australian effort was worthy in its endeavour but no more. Instead, there was a self-destruct element to much of the batting, with its roots, one hates to say, in one-day cricket, of which such a lot is played in the early part of the season. Three wickets, those of Chris Broad, Kim Barnett and Mike Gatting, fell in a morning session that yielded 88 runs from 28 overs. Then, in a frenetic afternoon, a further 124 came from 27 overs for the loss of Gooch, Gower, John Emburey and Robin Smith, who was playing in place of the injured Allan Lamb.

Nearly five runs per over and a wicket every half-hour. Great entertainment you might think, unless you have a ticket for Monday, but this is a Test match for goodness' sake, not a Sunday bun-fight, and 230 for 4, say, would have been infinitely preferable to 286 all out.

The three successes of the innings batted in contrasting styles. Gooch, by far the most consistent English batsman these days, has the phlegmatic, not to say dedicated, approach to a day's Test cricket that appears to have gone out of fashion in this country with Geoff Boycott. He spent hours in the nets on Wednesday ironing out what he feels is a worrying on-side fault and indeed, there is something of Boycott in the way he has rationalised his game from its thunderous youth, eliminating error and frippery in favour of occupation of the crease. By the time he was out, pushing uncharacteristically at a wide-ish ball from Waugh, he had hit nine boundaries, and not given the slightest hint of discomfort or error.

He had already seen the back of Broad, lbw to Alderman (who incidentally walked the tightrope of two official warnings from umpire Nigel Plews for running on the pitch); Barnett, caught at short leg having been driven cleverly back by Hughes, cheesed off no doubt by the batsman's horrible front-foot plonking even before the ball has left the hand; and Gatting, on his return to the fold, similarly taken, off bat and pad by Boon, first ball – a nightmare for a player whose place, in any case, was hard to justify on current form.

Gower, by contrast to Gooch, was for a while scintillating rather than safe, helped by a let-off when 7, hooking straight to long leg only for Dean Jones to spill the catch. Had that been held, England would have been in dire straits at 75 for 4, and Gower, who had been set up to play the shot, about ready for the hangman. Instead, it fired him up, and after adding 73 with

Scoreboard from Lord's

England won toss

England

First Innings

		6s	4s	Mins	Balls
G A Gooch c Healy b Waugh	60	–	9	167	123
B C Broad lbw b Alderman	18	–	3	54	45
K J Barnett c Boon b Hughes	14	–	2	30	24
M W Gatting c Boon b Hughes	0	–	–	6	1
*D I Gower b Lawson	57	–	8	105	62
R A Smith c Hohns b Lawson	32	–	6	52	36
J E Emburey b Alderman	0	–	–	3	2
†R C Russell not out	64	–	9	160	115
N A Foster c Jones b Hughes	16	–	3	56	51
P W Jarvis c Marsh b Hughes	6	–	1	16	14
G R Dilley c Border b Alderman	7	–	–	69	51
Extras (lb 9, nb 3)	12				
Total (86.5 overs)	**286**				

FALL OF WICKETS: 1–31, 2–52, 3–58, 4–131, 5–180, 6–185, 7–191, 8–237, 9–253.
BOWLING: Alderman 20.5–4–60–3 (nb 1); Lawson 27–8–88–2; Hughes 23–6–71–4; Waugh 9–3–49–1 (nb 2); Hohns 7–3–9–0.

Australia

First Innings

		6s	4s	Mins	Balls
G R Marsh not out	3	–	–	5	5
M A Taylor not out	1	–	–	5	1
Extras	0				
Total (no wkt, 1 over)	**4**				

D C Boon, *A R Border, D M Jones, S R Waugh, †I A Healy, M G Hughes, G F Lawson, T V Hohns and T M Alderman to bat.
BOWLING: Dilley 1–0–4–0.

Umpires: H D Bird and N T Plews.

Gooch in 17 overs, he and Smith plundered 49 from 7 more, with Smith merciless on some dross from Waugh.

Now this was wonderful entertainment, and if bad balls are bowled then they deserve the treatment no matter what the state or status of the game. But occasionally, as yesterday, players get caught up in the fervour, and the head no longer rules. So Gower, after a 54-ball half-century, dragged an attempted cut onto his stumps, Smith pulled a bouncer to mid-on, and Emburey completed a good day for Middlesex by being bowled second ball.

At this point, Russell took a hand. The Australians, whose imaginative field-placing so far in the series shows homework well done, believe him to be vulnerable to the short ball – not without good reason if Headingley is anything to go by – and didn't stint in offering it. Russell though, anticipating such treatment, has also worked hard in practice and was able to make sufficient room to cut and carve, and then when given the chance, to drive as sweetly as anything all day. Had he enjoyed the sort of responsible help from the lower order that Dilley showed at the death, he might well have gone on to greater things than just top scoring. Instead Foster, after being hit in the face by a bouncer from Hughes when late on a hook, tried another, connected perfectly this time, but succeeded only in helping it to Jones at long leg, who atoned for his earlier miss with a well-judged catch inches from the rope. Jarvis, who can be a decent player, also flung the bat brainlessly when circumspection was called for and when he was caught at gully, Russell might well have wondered whether it was all worth it.

Second Test, 2nd Day

England 286, Australia 276–6

This is a public health warning. The second day at Lord's has seen a severe outbreak of Test cricket as she is meant to be played, which could, unless a pretty sharp return is made to a proper diet of one-day cricket, prove terminally contagious. In perfect weather on a pitch to match, in front of a buzzing, babbling full house, Australia batted substantially better than England had done on the first day. But England, not to be outdone, raised their performance with the ball to levels not managed by Australia, showing in the process the sort of spirit and character that had been conspicuously absent at Headingley.

The upshot was that Australia advanced their overnight total of 4 for no wicket to 276 for 6 by the close of play, still 10 behind England, thanks mainly to a skilful, well-compiled and thoroughly professional 94 from David Boon, who has already shown a fondness for Lord's this season, and 62 from Mark Taylor, to leave him averaging 86 after his three innings so far in the series.

England employed four bowlers, Dilley, Foster, Jarvis and Emburey, during the day, and their effort, in much more trying conditions for them, put the performance at Leeds into its true perspective; one hopes, in view of the reluctance of some to accept criticism, in their own eyes as well. Dilley's return has added bite to the attack and he bowled well with the new ball, removing Geoff Marsh to a tumbling catch by Jack Russell in the day's fourth over and coming back strongly at the end, while Foster, obviously nervous and out of sorts at the start (Lord's is not his favourite test ground), recovered his rhythm and confidence once he changed to the Nursery end for an unbroken spell of 17 overs either side of tea, which helped put the game back in the balance. John Emburey was more his old self, too, for once looking as if he could take wickets, particularly when bowling to the left-handed Taylor, while Paul Jarvis will bowl worse for greater reward than the single wicket of Healy at the end of the day.

It was a marvellous day of ebb and flow. Australia, no doubt realising that it was largely due to the philanthropy of the England batsmen on Thursday that they were even batting, set out to make a solid base from which to take advantage and build a formidable first innings total, and after Dilley's early probing, Taylor and Boon, without so much as lip service to risk or frivolity, compiled a second-wicket partnership of 145 during which the only appeal of consequence was a loudspeaker one for the Bishop of Croydon. It was not broken until 20 minutes before tea when Foster, having begun his marathon spell, forced Taylor onto the back foot, and trapped him leg-before.

Even so, at 151 for 2 Australia were in the ascendant, and might have expected to take full toll of weary bowlers during the foot-slogging final session. Instead, as Australia pressed, England kept their heads up, worried and harried

LEFT Mike Gatting's return to Test cricket – and he is out first ball. Boon takes the catch

RIGHT Jack Russell to the rescue in England's first innings at Lord's – not for the last time

ABOVE Despair for Dilley as Australia's batsmen pile on the agony

BELOW On his way to another unbeaten hundred – Australia's Steve Waugh

Scoreboard from Lord's

England

First Innings: 286 (R C Russell 64 not out, G A Gooch 60, D I Gower 57; M G Hughes 4 for 71).

Australia

First Innings

	6s	4s	Mins	Balls
G R Marsh c Russell b Dilley..........	3	–	–	19	14
M A Taylor lbw b Foster.................	62	–	8	223	162
D C Boon c Gooch b Dilley	94	–	12	253	189
*A R Border c Smith b Emburey.....	35	–	5	81	62
D M Jones lbw b Foster	27	–	1	46	30
S R Waugh not out	35	–	5	66	64
†I A Healy c Russell b Jarvis..........	3	–	–	39	30
M G Hughes not out	2	–	–	9	4
Extras (lb 8, nb 7)	15				
Total (6 wkts, 91 overs)	**276**				

G F Lawson, T V Hohns and T M Alderman to bat.
FALL OF WICKETS: 1–6, 2–151, 3–192, 4–221, 5–235, 6–265.
BOWLING: Dilley 17–2–71–2 (nb 9); Foster 29–7–68–2; Jarvis 19–3–69–1; Emburey 26–6–60–1 (nb 1).

them like dogs after a rat, and were rewarded with the vital wickets of Boon, Border and Dean Jones, so that at 235 for 5 now, and a new ball looming, the prospect faced Australia of not even taking a first innings lead at all; the balance of power had shifted. After Healy's departure, Hughes and Steve Waugh, looking ominous on 35, were compelled to cling on, surviving in the process one over of the second new ball. It will now be down to the Australian tail to support Waugh as the England tail might have backed Russell.

The innings of the match so far came from Boon, this four-square gum-chewing figure, capped rather than helmeted, now so much a symbol of Australian pugnacity, who has come a million miles since the uncertain days when not even an A–Z of the crease could have told him where his off-stump was. His innings yesterday was beautifully paced: 50 from 94 balls, and 189 balls in all, with a dozen boundaries, none better than his first, a cover-drive off Dilley as crisp as a new tenner, and later a brutal square cut off the same flagging bowler. There were only two moments of perceptible trouble for him. At 53, Barnett missed him at backward point as he drove rashly at a wider ball from Jarvis, and earlier the same bowler had picked up two points for a cannon off a pair of pinks that might have felled an ox: his discomfort was obvious.

Boon, whose entire family apparently had arrived that day – how inconsiderate of him to spend so much time in the middle – deserved a century and few would have begrudged it. Instead, Dilley, world-weary but game, flogged one more delivery out of the pitch, saw Boon reach and edge outside off-stump and Gooch, with not a hint of fuss, pouched the catch at second slip.

It heralded England's best spell of the game, with Foster and Emburey wheeling away in tandem. Border, whose brisk 35 was a characteristically brave attempt to break the stranglehold, swept Embury, perhaps off glove, to short fine leg where Smith had been placed for that very purpose, and Jones, running like a stag and looking ominously well set, was caught half-forward to Foster and was out lbw.

Second Test, 3rd Day

England 286 and 58–3, Australia 528

When Geoff Lawson plucked Chris Broad's off-stump from the ground late on the afternoon of the 3rd day, those at Lord's would have been forgiven for expecting the jangle of the bedside alarm to announce that breakfast and papers were awaiting and Australia were still 276 for 6. In cricketing terms, if you are English that is, this Saturday had been the worst of all possible nightmares: such a stark contrast to the marvellous fight-back of the previous day as to defy belief.

Before play, one might well have assumed that Australia would take the lead and probably top 300. At a pinch 350 was a possibility if someone could defy the new ball and stay long enough with Steve Waugh. But if you had suggested 528 as the final score, the white coats would have been rapidly on the scene. The loss of the three cheap wickets in the evening should come as no surprise when a side has been sandbagged like that.

It was a magnificent effort from Waugh and the Australian tail of Merv Hughes, Geoff Lawson and Terry Alderman, all of whom amply demonstrated what might have been possible if the English tail, or recognised batsmen for that matter, had shown the same regard for occupation of the crease. Waugh did not play as fluently as he had at Headingley, and his stealthy creep through the nineties suggested that he knew the importance of this second hundred not only to his side but also to dispel any doubts in his mind – no one else can surely have harboured any – that his century in Leeds might have been a glorious but singular jewel. Before play, Allan Border, whose stature as captain grows daily, had told his man that if he were to get out then to make sure he was the last. The support he got was so good that he was able to play it exactly as he wanted, the need to farm the bowling eliminated. Indeed so much did Lawson take charge of the early part of their 130-run stand that Waugh was able to reach his hundred without fuss or anxiety and then take a mental breather while the bowler scored 50 of the first 67 added.

Having said how well Australia played, however, charges now have to be laid at the England door, and particularly that of the captain David Gower. Throughout the day, England undeniably suffered the most appalling luck. But if you base your whole strategy on whether the dice rolls for you and leave it at that, then things have come to a sorry pass, for however fortune treats you, it is possible to at least maximise your chances of it changing, by employing plain, simple common sense, rather than the 'instinct' on which Gower professes to rely.

The performance of the England captain on the field on Saturday was as unhappy an exhibition of captaincy as those watching – and there were many who have seen an awful lot of Test cricket – can remember. Simply put, Gower lost control, or his marbles or both, when things

started to go wrong. At one point, with Gower looking a pathetic, lonely figure, it seemed that Mike Gatting had actually taken it upon himself to run things.

Most of the criticism can be centred around Gower's handling of his bowlers. He was unable to explain, except to suggest that it was the 'better end to bowl', why Foster, who had bowled so valiantly from the Nursery end on Friday to help wrest the initiative from Australia, was allowed to plug away from the Pavilion end for 90 fruitless minutes after his initial new ball dart, and even returned there after lunch for 45 minutes more. Whether or not he ought to be able to bowl from that end, it is so patently obvious that it can upset his rhythm – he was twice warned for running on the pitch – and that the Nursery end by contrast brings the best out of him. You could almost swear it was a juvenile and futile effort to prove a point. Meanwhile Jarvis, whose method and preference demands the Pavilion, and who bowls well from there, followed Dilley at the Nursery. It was baffling.

So was the use of Emburey, England's tightest bowler, who conceded eight boundaries in 42 overs (Jarvis went for 23), and whose parsimony eventually brought its belated rewards. It hardly seems worth mentioning that Gooch, whose bowling, it was grandly announced before the match, figured strongly in the plans, was eventually given his chance after 141 overs with the score 494 for 8: he didn't concede a single boundary in his six overs.

This game, and indeed the series, is not yet over and should England sneak ahead, the Australians will be haunted by some bad memories of chasing low totals to win. But it is possible that Gower's lack of leadership when the chips were down may have already cost England the Ashes.

He should not be condemned entirely alone though, even though as captain he takes both plaudits and brickbats. Gower makes no secret of the fact that he captains by committee, so where were the committee on Saturday? Can Gooch, who is Foster's county captain, not have seen what was happening to his bowler? Does Gatting not know Lord's well enough to see what was going on? Was Emburey, an England

ABOVE High scoring from Australia's tail-enders was a feature of the series. Here Geoff Lawson sweeps his way to a fine 74

RIGHT Foster's dejection is obvious as, not for the first time, he struggles from the Pavilion End at Lord's

Gower pushes a reluctant Foster towards the Pavilion End (LEFT) but runs into trouble explaining this to the Press afterwards (BELOW). He was heavily criticised for cutting short the Press conference

Scoreboard from Lord's

England

First Innings: 286 (R C Russell 64 not out, G A Gooch 60, D I Gower 57; M G Hughes 4 for 71).

Second Innings

	6s	4s	Mins	Balls
G A Gooch lbw b Alderman	0	–	–	2	3
B C Broad b Lawson	20	–	4	44	30
K J Barnett c Jones b Alderman......	3	–	–	31	21
M W Gatting not out	16	–	3	66	51
*D I Gower not out	15	–	2	53	33
Extras (lb 4)	4				
Total (3 wkts, 23 overs)	**58**				

R A Smith, J E Emburey, †R C Russell, P W Jarvis, N A Foster and G R Dilley to bat.

FALL OF WICKETS: 1–0, 2–18, 3–28.
BOWLING: Alderman 8–2–23–2; Lawson 9–3–21–1; Hughes 4–2–8–0; Border 2–1–2–0.

Australia

First innings

	6s	4s	Mins	Balls
G R Marsh c Russell b Dilley..........	3	–	–	19	14
M A Taylor lbw b Foster.................	62	–	8	223	162
D C Boon c Gooch b Dilley	94	–	12	253	189
*A R Border c Smith b Emburey.....	35	–	5	81	62
D M Jones lbw b Foster	27	–	1	46	30
S R Waugh not out	152	–	17	329	249
†I A Healy c Russell b Jarvis...........	3	–	–	39	30
M G Hughes c Gooch b Foster	30	–	4	71	52
T V Hohns b Emburey	21	–	3	52	38
G F Lawson c Broad b Emburey.....	74	–	11	107	94
T M Alderman lbw b Emburey	8	–	1	36	39
Extras (lb 11, nb 8)	19				
Total (158 overs)	**528**				

FALL OF WICKETS: 1–6, 2–151, 3–192, 4–221, 5–235, 6–265, 7–331, 8–381, 9–511.
BOWLING: Dilley 34–3–141–2 (nb 10); Foster 45–7–129–3; Jarvis 31–3–150–1; Emburey 42–12–88–4 (nb 1); Gooch 6–2–9–0.

captain himself last year and not a bad one, even asked what he thought? Maybe they all offered advice and it was rejected, in which case Gower is a fool. And finally, as the glib answer is always that things always look easier from the stands, where does Micky Stewart, who spends his time in that position, fit into all this?

Gower's subsequent and uncharacteristic rudeness at the later press conference can be if not excused then at least explained as that of a bloke near the end of his tether rather than someone anxious to catch a cab to a show: there are other cabs. He has apologised, probably at the instigation of Ted Dexter, who said yesterday that having agreed before the series to give the press conferences, he ought then to give them his full attention, and that Gower had been reminded of this. Gower is the representative of the team, and while it carries its rewards in many ways, there are responsibilities as well which, however fraught he may be, have to be endured. His golden image has been left a little tarnished.

Second Test, 4th Day

England 286 and 322–9, Australia 528

Barring bad weather, or the sort of miracle from the one remaining England wicket that winkles enough runs to cause a few blushes, Australia will win the second Test on the final day, take a 2–0 lead in the six-Test series and thereby become the first Australian side since Bradman's 1948 crew to win consecutive Tests in England.

With 58 on the board, England began the fourth day with 184 still needed to make Australia bat again, three top-order batsmen out, and a captain aware that the tabloids were already calling for his head after Saturday's fiasco. They lost Mike Gatting after fifty minutes, but then prospered as David Gower, batting under more pressure than he ever can have done, and Robin Smith put together a stand of 139 which took England through almost until tea-time. Gower, appropriately with the Queen's Monday tea-time visit impending, made a quite majestic 106, his first Test century for almost three years and his fifteenth in all, before falling to Merv Hughes, while Smith, four agonising runs short of what would have been his maiden Test century, went to the new ball, brilliantly exploited once more by Terry Alderman. Four of the six wickets to fall during the day went to

Alderman, giving him 6 for 111 in the innings so far and 19 wickets already in the series, putting him well on the way to the 42 he took here in 1981. The new ball also did for Jack Russell, Neil Foster and Paul Jarvis and England finished the day at 322 for 9, just 80 runs ahead. But there was fight in the side yesterday which was never apparent at Headingley, and things were never handed on a plate to the Australian bowlers.

Realistically, it was always unlikely that England would be able to bat for two days to save the game, but curiously, if they could have managed a lead of say 150, it would not, class of '81 may recall, be outside the realms of possibility that on a wearing pitch with their dander up they could still have given Australia a scare or even won, although Gower is no sorcerer like Brearley and the apprentice still kicks his heels in Worcester.

Major contributions had to come from the three remaining batsmen and resilience from the tail, but it wasn't to be Gatting's day. He'd played himself in quietly and studiously enough when suddenly, perhaps because he hadn't done it for three innings, he shouldered arms to Alderman, the ball darted back, and Dickie Bird, who is scarcely the man from Del Monte when it comes to answering lbw shouts, gave him unhesitatingly out.

There was almost an air of inevitability about Gower's hundred, following the events of Saturday. He is not daft enough to think that batting well as he did in any way exonerates his lackadaisical captaincy, but it showed his mettle. From the off, his footwork, often not his strongest point, was purposeful and his timing through the off-side exquisite. Aberrations were few: just an airy one-handed waft down the leg-side early on that was closer to the ball than he may have liked, and a chance cut hard to gully when he had made 26, which Marsh held and then dropped, – as he sportingly indicated as he tumbled over – and a bit of streakiness in the 80s. But when he pushed the single to mid-on that brought him his hundred after four and a quarter hours, a packed, sympathetic Lord's rose to him like an Atlantic swell.

Unfortunately for him, the Queen had arrived to see it and the advent of Royalty has been

Scoreboard from Lord's

England

First Innings: 286 (R C Russell 64 not out, G A Gooch 60, D I Gower 57; M G Hughes 4 for 71).

Second Innings

	6s	4s	Mins	Balls
G A Gooch lbw b Alderman	0	–	–	2	3
B C Broad b Lawson	20	–	4	44	30
K J Barnett c Jones b Alderman......	3	–	–	31	21
M W Gatting lbw Alderman	22	–	4	114	82
*D I Gower c Border b Hughes.......	106	–	16	268	198
R A Smith b Alderman	96	–	16	269	206
†R C Russell c Boon b Lawson	29	–	4	71	65
J E Emburey not out	21	–	2	73	44
N A Foster lbw Alderman	4	–	1	3	2
P W Jarivs lbw b Alderman	5	–	–	19	16
G R Dilley not out	4	–	1	17	14
Extras (lb 5, b 5, nb 2)................	12				
Total (9 wkts, 113 overs)	**322**				

FALL OF WICKETS: 1–0, 2–18, 3–28, 4–84, 5–223, 6–274, 7–300, 8–304, 9–314.
BOWLING: Alderman 34–6–111–6; Lawson 32–9–89–2 (nb 2); Hughes 22–7–40–1 (nb 1); Border 9–3–23–0; Hohns 12–5–33–0; Waugh 4–1–16–0.

Australia

First Innings: 528 (M A Taylor 62, D C Boon 94, S R Waugh 152 not out, G F Lawson 74; J E Emburey 4 for 88).

regarded as the equivalent of a nifty bowling change ever since George V dismissed Ponsford with a fleeting visit here in 1930. Merv Hughes, who was in the middle of a mightily impressive hostile spell that included a warning from umpire Nigel Plews for overdoing the short stuff, bounced one more at Gower who, unable to keep it down, fended it to Border at backward short leg. Later, when the teams were introduced to her, Gower was seen deep in conversation with the Queen, who was either apologising for the untimely intrusion or more likely just wanted to know why Foster didn't bowl from the Nursery end on Saturday. Smith meanwhile was pugnacious and, quite rightly, not afraid to hammer the bad ball with drives and cuts in spite of the situation. Pertinently though, in view of next winter's tour to the West Indies, he does commit to the front foot and Hughes was not backward

A rueful smile from Dickie Bird, up goes the finger, and Alderman claims yet another lbw victim

LEFT Time England had a new captain? But Dickie Bird is only telling David Gower to hurry things along as Australia head for victory on the final day

The end of Mike Gatting's second innings at Lord's – and possibly the last Test innings of his career

Jubilant Australian slips acclaim another wicket

in spotting this, giving him a terrible roasting which Smith did well to survive.

The new ball, delayed by Border for six overs in an effort to make a breakthrough without it and expose the tail, changed things. After he surprisingly let Waugh, at the bowler's instigation, have a couple of overs with it to round off a spell, Lawson got his hands on it and Russell, who had again played pleasantly, flipped a catch from bat and pad which Boon took at the batsman's feet. Then Smith, confidently approaching his century, leaned forward and Alderman drifted one languidly past his outside edge to clip the off stump: the delivery of the series without a shadow of a doubt. Foster and Jarvis both added themselves to the ever-growing list of Alderman lbw victims – over half his wickets, so far this series have come in this manner – before Emburey and Dilley saw out the day.

Second Test, 5th Day

England 286, and 359
Australia 528, and 119–4
Australia won by 6 wickets

When, shortly before five o'clock, Steve Waugh forced a short ball from Paul Jarvis away to the cover boundary for the runs which won the second Test for Australia, it put one antipodean hand more than tenuously on the Ashes urn.

If notice is taken of history, Australia's excellent 6-wicket win, achieved ultimately not only against England but the weather as well, gives David Gower's side little chance of coming back in the series. Only once, when Bradman's Australians conceded the first two matches to Gubby Allen's 1937–38 tourists, has a side rallied to win a series from being two down, and England's best effort against anyone from that deficit was when Len Hutton managed, 35 years ago, to

draw a series in the Caribbean. Gower, of course needs only similarly to draw to retain the Ashes, and the fact that there are six Tests in the series is in his favour from that viewpoint – although he might regret it if Australia are 5–0 up after five – but with Australia on such a mighty roll, it is asking a lot.

England's only realistic chance of saving the game rested, as Gower conceded, with the Met Office. Rain showers were forecast, but although dark, brooding clouds duly materialised in the vicinity of St John's Wood, the only moisture of consequence fell in an impenetrable sheet during the lunch interval, which as Gower said, was a waste: like mugging someone on their way into the bank. It delayed the restart by three-quarters of an hour, but thereafter never threatened and ultimately ceased to become an issue.

That Australia had been set 118 to win, more than they would have liked, was down to John Emburey and Graham Dilley, who with common sense, straight bats, a bit of nudging and nurdling, and a couple of forthright blows from Dilley, extended their frustrating last wicket stand to 45, the England score from 322 to 359, and importantly used up a further hour in the process, before Dilley edged a bat and pad catch to Boon, which is rapidly becoming as popular a way for England batsmen to get out as being lbw to Terry Alderman.

It was just enough perhaps to put Australian nerves on edge – copies of the 1982 *Wisden*, with its reports of Headingley and Birmingham 1981 when they failed to chase targets of 130 and 151 respectively, will have been banned from the dressing room. This was a better pitch though, and the only dilemma would have been between the need on one hand to pace the innings without undue risk which might, had it rained enough, have left them short, and the desire to crack on a bit in view of the forecast, with the consequent risk of losing wickets and the weather staying fine.

As it was, Australia did get themselves into something of a hole, losing four wickets for 67 before tea, a direct result of a combination of Australian aggression and a 3 for 2 spell in 11 balls from Neil Foster – from the Pavilion end it scarcely need be said. It was a noble effort

Scoreboard from Lord's

England

First Innings: 286 (G A Gooch 60, D I Gower 57, R C Russell 64 not out; M G Hughes 4 for 71).

Second Innings

	6s	4s	Mins	Balls
G A Gooch lbw b Alderman	0	–	2	3
B C Broad b Lawson	20	–	4	44	30
K J Barnett c Jones b Alderman......	3	–	31	21
M W Gatting lbw Alderman	22	–	4	114	82
*D I Gower c Border b Hughes......	106	–	16	268	198
R A Smith b Alderman	96	–	16	269	206
†R C Russell c Boon b Lawson	29	–	4	71	65
J E Emburey not out	36	–	4	137	96
N A Foster lbw b Alderman	4	–	1	3	2
P W Jarvis lbw b Alderman	5	–	19	16
G R Dilley c Boon b Hughes...........	24	–	3	81	64
Extras (lb 6, b 6, nb 2)................	14				
Total (130 overs)	**359**				

FALL OF WICKETS: 1–0, 2–18, 3–28, 4–84, 5–223, 6–274, 7–300, 8–304, 9–314.
BOWLING: Alderman 38–6–128–6; Lawson 39–10–99–2 (nb 2); Hughes 24–8–44–2 (nb 1); Border 9–3–23–0; Hohns 13–6–33–0; Waugh 7–2–20–0.

Australia

First Innings: 528 (M A Taylor 62, D C Boon 94, S R Waugh 152 not out, G F Lawson 74; J E Emburey 4 for 88).

Second Innings

	6s	4s	Mins	Balls
M A Taylor c Gooch b Foster.........	27	–	2	78	61
G R Marsh b Dilley	1	–	–	17	12
D C Boon not out	58	–	6	157	121
*A R Border c sub (R Sims) b Foster	1	–	–	15	9
D M Jones c Russell b Foster.........	0	–	–	8	4
S R Waugh not out	21	–	2	69	40
Extras (b 3, lb 4, nb 4)................	11				
Total (4 wkts, 40.2 overs)	**119**				

†I A Healy, M G Hughes, G F Lawson, T V Hohns and T M Alderman did not bat.
FALL OF WICKETS: 1–9, 2–51, 3–61, 4–67.
BOWLING: Dilley 10–2–27–1 (nb 5); Foster 18–3–39–3; Emburey 3–0–8–0; Jarvis 9.2–0–38–0.
Man of the match: S R Waugh.

Australia won by 6 wickets.

from the Essex seamer, who did so much to claw England back into contention on Friday. It may have helped him knowing that the job was to contain and hope the rain came, rather than all-

out attack – both umpires spoke to Gower about time-wasting in that regard but it was more a gesture than anything, and one can't blame Gower for slowing things down – but his control was such that Gower was fully justified in keeping him going for 18 overs at the end from which he struggled on Saturday. Maybe he was straining too hard then.

Before Foster's intervention, Mark Taylor and Boon, with a stand of 42, had made a steady recovery from the early loss of Geoff Marsh who, with nine on the board, embarrassingly shouldered arms to Dilley and lost his off-stump. But Foster reintroduced the jitters. First Taylor, on 27, his first score under 60 in the series, edged to Gooch at second slip who scooped and claimed a low catch. The batsman waited for the umpires to confer as to whether it had carried rather than take Gooch's word, which may have been a dig at Foster who hadn't taken Dean Jones' word for a boundary catch on the first afternoon. A pity: out of such are vendettas made.

Border, his concentration broken perhaps by the previous ball which slipped from Foster's hand and bounced twice onto his pad, then pulled a short ball straight to an 18-year-old groundstaff boy, Robin Sims, fielding at long leg as substitute for the injured Robin Smith. He confidently made a catch he'll remember, throwing it up self-consciously as if remembering where he was. Border later caught up with him in the dressing room, ruffled his hair and called him something believed to be an Aussie term of endearment.

When, with tea imminent, Jones mishooked a bouncer and Russell made ground to take the catch, doubts could have set in, and Border, in a rash of superstition that seizes cricketers on these occasions, was banished to the showers to suffer the wait alone.

But the sky was clearing now and the need to rush had receded. Boon and Steve Waugh pushed their singles, dispatched the occasional bad ball for four, and eased Australia steadily to the target. There was just one more jitter, when Waugh, on 11, was missed at point by Broad off the unfortunate Jarvis, whose figures in the match have been positively Pringly, but by then the match was won and lost. Boon was able to complete his fifty, to go with his 94 in the first innings, before Waugh stroked the winning runs. He has now made 350 runs in this series without being dismissed. A hundred years ago a chap called Bates played for England against Australia; no one of that name has played Test cricket since. 'Blaster' of that ilk might well be the next for England's only hope now seems to be to dynamite Waugh from the crease.

Postscript

The second Test, on their favourite ground, was an Australian triumph which put the shambles of Headingley into true perspective. True credit, they felt, had not been given to Border and his team for a fine performance, with the accent on English failings. But there, England's performance was so pitiful that the Australians scarcely had to raise their game. An ordinary side beat an abject one.

At Lord's, England, who played rather better than they had done in Leeds, were beaten by a side which raised its game, as a team, to levels which nobody before the tour can have conceived. Now credit can be given to Australia: each side would have trounced their Headingley counterparts.

In the crucial first innings, England batted like millionaires while Australia, having seen the charity dispensed, played like misers tucking the pennies away under the mattress for second innings rainy days. Boon, Taylor, Hughes and later Lawson all contributed handsomely but once more, the performance of Waugh was astonishing. He is so correct – right forward or right back and no half measures. He drives squarer than one might like, but it's done with the blade angled, never cross-batted. And the square drive off the back foot has received the accolade of a boundary fielder to cope with it. How fitting that he should be the one to steer Australia calmly home when it looked as if the

weather might rob them. 350 runs now in three knocks, without being dismissed is unbelievable.

But England were outplayed in other areas too. That Australia reached 528 was largely due not so much to how England's bowlers performed – by and large the best available, they were a vast improvement on Headingley – but to how they were asked to bowl; not on Friday, which will long be remembered as Test cricket par excellence, but on Saturday when England squandered the ground they had fought so hard to gain. The debate will roll on about Gower's handling of them – should Foster have had the Nursery end, or was it right to persist with him at the Pavilion end? The persistence appeared to pay off, but not until the second innings when it was too late – but there can be no doubt that they were not given the best chance. Emburey for instance, who, apart from Foster's brave Friday effort, looked by far the most effective bowler, bowled his 42 overs in seven spells, clearly as an alternative to seam and no more. It is hoped that this much at least has been noted: that even if England are blind to it – with some justification given Emburey's recent Test history – Australia are more than aware of the danger that lurks there.

What of Gower now? He has been outgunned by Border who is looking a captain of real authority. Everything he tries at present is working of course, and the job is easy on those terms, but he shows a flair and executive ability that Gower seems to lack. Border could fall of course, and inventive field-placings look ridiculous then, but one feels Gower could never reach these heights. So it made his century all the more memorable, for it demonstrated his steel as a batsman. Wistful ability is not enough without determination, and Gower, batting under extreme pressure, was exceptional. He knew that he had made mistakes and that self esteem for his side and himself could only be clawed back with the bat. It was a memorable moment when the crowd rose to him and while it doesn't make him a better captain, that one innings, maybe the best of his life, makes him a man.

Finally there was once more Alderman. It was believed by many that Alderman, should they keep him fit, could hold the key to the series.

There is a long way to go yet, but he has already won two Test matches for his side, brilliantly exploiting English batting deficiencies, winning lbw decision after decision. His 19-wicket haul thus far means that he has now taken 61 in seven matches in this country.

It would be wrong for England to panic just yet with the team for the third Test. The message might well be 'same players, but pull your fingers out'. Australia are on a phenomenal roll, and success with touring sides in general, and Aussies in particular, breeds more of it. The change had better come soon, though.

Third Cornhill Test Match

England v Australia, Edgbaston, 6−11 July 1989

Match preview

Just when you really need them on your side, there are times in sport when the odds and gods simply turn their backs on you. England's position in this six-match Ashes series is not yet desperate, but at 2–0 down with four to play, this Third Test at Edgbaston could be the last chance to claw something back against an Australian side with confidence generating like a nuclear reactor.

Yet throughout the series the methods England have chosen to counter it, whether or not one agrees with them, have been consistently thwarted to the extent that so far, they have been unable, through injury, to field the side they initially selected, and this Test has already proved no different. Already deprived of both Allan Lamb (for the second Test running) and Robin Smith, and probably Neil Foster as well, they were dealt a further blow when Mike Gatting, in the course of a routine phone call home before practice on Wednesday afternoon, learned of the sudden death of his mother-in-law, and immediately returned to London. Chris Tavaré of Somerset, who has not played a Test match since facing Sri Lanka in 1984 – ironically the low-point of David Gower's first spell as England captain – was immediately invited to join the squad.

In purely pragmatic terms, Tavaré replacing Gatting would be no bad thing. The Middlesex captain has not had the best of playing times recently with only 42 runs from his last six knocks, including a dreadful return to Test cricket at Lord's. In addition there has been an obvious need for a player not to blaze away, but he prepared single-mindedly to occupy the crease, a quality absent, Gooch excepted, in the first two Tests.

In county cricket, Tavaré has always been a dominant player; a strokemaker up there with the best at times, and this season, as if to emphasise the point, he has, since his move to Taunton from Kent, scored five centuries in first-class cricket, four of them in limited overs games. No slouch this. Unless, that is, you transpose him into Test cricket. Then, if it's pure unmitigated boredom you want, Tavaré's your man: a person who can make Night Nurse seem like happy water. The transformation from one persona to the other can be astonishing and is merely a function of the man's capacity to adapt to the needs of the side as he sees them.

The Australians have not escaped the Tavaré torpor. Try this for size: after two unsuccessful Tests in 1980 against West Indies, he was recalled for the Fifth Test against Australia at Manchester the following year, and marked it with a display of such stupendous somnambulance that innings of 69 and 78 saw him spend a total of very nearly 12 hours at the crease, including on the way, at 306 minutes, the slowest fifty in English first-class cricket. On another occasion in Perth, in the course of the same innings he went scoreless for more than an hour, not once, but twice for heaven's sake. The mouth is already watering at what he might have in store for us here.

Like Headingley, Edgbaston has in the past not been the happiest hunting ground for Australia, ever since 1902 when they made only 36, their lowest-ever score in a Test. There were no matches between the sides here between 1909 and 1961 but only once in seven games – 1975 when captain Mike Denness made a crucial cock-up with the toss – have Australia won. They might have done in 1981 when set to make 151 to win, but one I T Botham managed to take five wickets for one run in 28 balls and that was that. Four years later, he walked to the middle, with Gower, Gatting and Robinson already having made hundreds, and smote the first ball he received from Craig McDermott over the pavilion. Goodness knows what's up his sleeve this time, but for England's sake there'd better be something good.

Third Test, 1st day

Australia 232–4

For a moment it had all gone according to script. At precisely six minutes past midday, Ian Botham, who like Pilgrim has suffered setbacks to his career that might have seen off fainter-hearted folk, finally got the chance to bowl once more in the Eternal City of a Test match. His first delivery for almost two years, a slow-medium loosener, swung gently into the left-handed Mark Taylor like wind-blown gossamer, pitched, continued off the seam and thudded into the batsman's pads. Bowler, slips, the whole ground yelled their tonsils out. Then a strange thing

happened: Dickie Bird shook his head and gave the batsman not out.

This is not the sort of thing we expect from Botham comebacks. Hadn't he so mesmerised Bruce Edgar first ball on his return from a ban a couple of years ago that he edged a catch to slip. A master of timing. 'Who writes your scripts?' Graham Gooch, the juggling catcher, had asked. But Botham then with the ball was cricket's Indiana Jones, swash-and-buckling his buccaneering way through the best batting in the world. He has a different script writer now though; his bowling is more methodically precise – slower, dainty even, and disciplined.

For a while yesterday it served England well. David Gower had elected not to win the toss for the eleventh consecutive time, and Border, who is not used to having to make such decisions, chose to bat first. Marsh and Taylor hared away, mostly at the expense of Paul Jarvis, and after 15 overs had made 48. First point to Australia.

But long, attritional spells by Botham (1 for 50) and John Emburey (2 for 51 from 25 overs), well-supported on his debut by Angus Fraser, who, although wicketless, can be well satisfied with his 14 overs for 26 runs, definitely gave the next point to England as three wickets fell in the hour after lunch, and only 57 runs had been added in 30 overs. Australia, at 105 for 3, were in some bother.

They needn't have worried. By the time play ended three-quarters of an hour early, through bad light initially and then Wagnerian thunder, lightning and rain of a tropical intensity which flooded the ground in ten minutes, Dean Jones, with 71 not out, David Boon, who made 38 easy runs before being unluckily run out, and later Steve Waugh, who is, of course, not out and the ball already striking a tattoo on the middle of his bat, had seen them to 232 for 4. The new ball is due in two overs' time and could change everything, but the day on balance was just Australia's.

Without doubt, England's best spell followed a brief post-lunch period where after much introspection, it looked like Geoff Marsh and Mark Taylor could romp away. But Botham and

Botham's back – and his first ball brought this confident appeal

The moment England thought would never arrive – Steve Waugh is dismissed for the first time in the series, bowled by Angus Fraser

RIGHT Dean Jones stepped smartly into Waugh's shoes to hit an exciting 157

Scoreboard from Edgbaston

Australia won toss

Australia

First Innings

	6s	4s	Mins	Balls
G R Marsh lbw Botham	42	–	2	145	134
M A Taylor st Russell b Emburey...	43	–	5	135	99
D C Boon run out (Jarvis)..............	38	–	5	134	111
*A R Border b Embury	8	–	1	17	21
D M Jones not out	71	–	7	149	118
S R Waugh not out	17	–	3	42	29
Extras (lb 5, nb 8)	13			
Total (4 wkts, 83.3 overs)	**232**			

†I A Healy, T V Hohns, M G Hughes, G F Lawson and T M Alderman to bat.
FALL OF WICKETS: 1–88, 2–94, 3–105, 4–201.
BOWLING: Dilley 10–1–39–0 (nb 8); Jarvis, 15–3–61–0; Fraser 14–3–26–0 (nb 3); Botham 19.3–5–50–1; Embury 25–4–51–2.

England

G A Gooch, T S Curtis, K J Barnett, C J Tavaré, *D I Gower, I T Botham, †R C Russell, J E Emburey, A R C Fraser, P W Jarvis and G R Dilley.

Umpires: H D Bird and J W Holder.

Emburey hauled England back in the space of eight overs. These have not been happy years for Emburey, who increasingly has felt that his role has been interpreted as that of stock bowler rather than bona fide attacker. But although his confidence and rhythm suffered accordingly and his trajectory flattened – The Trader of the Lost Arc perhaps – there were signs at Lord's of a return to his best. He was twirling away 15 minutes before lunch, and so impressed Gower that he continued with him after the interval – an off-spinner . . . on the first day!

It brought rewards. With the score on 88, Taylor, who while looking a thoroughly competent opening bat against seam had appeared all at sea against the spinner, waltzed down the track, coinciding unfortunately with Emburey turning the first thing since his ankle in Karachi, and Russell completed a neat stumping; when did the first wicket of a Test last fall like that?

Three overs later, Botham, to everyone's delight but none more than his own, trapped Marsh lbw to a ball that preferred no obvious malice except a lethal quality of straightness. Was it ever so. Then at 105, Allan Border, who had just become only the fourth player to complete 8,000 runs in Test cricket, was somehow bowled round his legs by Emburey offering no shot – a little pad involved perhaps.

Nor had the wheel of England's good fortune finished turning just yet. Boon, pugnacious as ever, and Jones, an Indian wristiness in his play, had added 96 runs for the fourth wicket as easy as you like, with Jones already past a 76-ball fifty, when he laced a half volley from Jarvis, not exactly a rare commodity at the moment, back at the bowler who deflected the ball onto the stumps with Boon out of his ground. Jones hurled his bat down in anguish. England had better not complain about luck again.

Third Test, 2nd day

Australia 294–6

It had to happen. As forecast exclusively in a tabloid newspaper yesterday, Steve Waugh, after something like 13 hours at the crease finally acquired an average by getting out. He has made a grand total of 393 runs in the series so far, which is not quite the most ever made between dismissals – someone called Sobers in 1958 had consecutive innings of 365 not out and 125 against Pakistan – but it's not a bad effort.

The tabloid's further forecast that it would be Ian Botham, of course, who perpetrated the deed proved erroneous. It was a quarter past five on a murky Edgbaston evening when Angus Fraser, the pick, by some distance, of the English seamers, not only in this match but probably this summer, created a split-second of indecision in Waugh, darted the ball back off the seam inside a tentative forward prod – just about the first time that Waugh has been unsure of anything he has done – and knocked back the off stump. Waugh had made 43, and it was a strange sight to see him walk off the ground alone. Fraser, for all his size and undoubted ability, blushed almost shyly with the pleasure of this first Test wicket.

That there was any play at all yesterday was a tribute to the dear old Brumbrella, which kept at bay the thousands of gallons of water that fell on Thursday evening and throughout yesterday morning. It did not survive unscathed: when the rain finally ceased at half past three, and the process of rolling up the massive sheet began, it was discovered that the cylinder around which the cover winds, powered by motors, was all but severed in the middle. The decision to risk a complete breakdown during the removal process was taken, successfully fortunately, and the roller – actually a length of North Sea oil pipe – was taken to be welded overnight.

It meant that before the misty gloom blanketed the ground for good once more, 67 minutes of play were possible, in two sessions, during which Australia, in 15.3 overs, extended their overnight 232 for 4 by 62 runs to reach 294 for the additional loss of Waugh, after he and Jones had added 71 in 78 minutes, and Ian Healy for 2, also to Fraser. But there was also time for Dean Jones, 71 not out overnight, to stroke his way to his fifth Test century in 24 Tests and his second against England.

England's hopes of a breakthrough rested with the new ball which was available after nine balls. And who do you think took it? It really hasn't taken Ian Botham long to elevate himself from fourth to first seamer, and there is a school of thought which says why not give him a go. I bet it was his idea though, and not a great one at that given his pace now. As it turned out Botham, troubled by damp footholds, conceded runs from every ball – 11 in all from the first over, including a sumptuous cover drive from Waugh. With Dilley also wayward, runs were coming apace and the 50-stand was completed in 57 minutes.

After five overs and 25 runs, the intervention once more of bad light proved timely for it gave England the chance to have an urgent rethink of policy, with the brains trust arriving at the

Scoreboard from Edgbaston

Australia

First Innings

	6s	4s	Mins	Balls
G R Marsh lbw b Botham	42	–	–	145	134
M A Taylor st Russell b Emburey	43	–	2	135	99
D C Boon run out (Jarvis)	38	–	5	134	111
*A R Border b Emburey	8	–	5	17	21
D M Jones not out	101	–	11	216	167
S R Waugh b Fraser	43	–	6	78	54
†I A Healy b Fraser	2	–	–	16	12
M G Hughes not out	1	–	–	11	11
Extras (lb 7, nb 9)	16				
Total (6 wkts, 99 overs)	**294**				

T V Hohns, G F Lawson and T M Alderman to bat.
FALL OF WICKETS: 1–88, 2–94, 3–105, 4–201, 5–272, 6–289.
BOWLING: Dilley 18–1–80–0 (nb 12); Jarvis, 15–3–61–0; Fraser 19–6–30–2 (nb 3); Botham 22–5–65–1; Emburey 25–4–51–2.

unusual ploy of giving the new ball to their best bowler. It worked for a while. Dilley was providing the entertainment at one end – his first over back after the restart yielded a brace of off-side boundaries to Waugh, saw him beaten outside off-stump a couple of times and missed at gully by Gooch, and finished with a bouncer which sizzled Jones's nose hairs.

Fraser by contrast was a model of steadiness. There is much of Mike Hendrick in his high action and accuracy, and indeed, because he bowls a fuller length, he might prove a better Test wicket-taker. Accuracy, believe it or not, pays dividends and this is not a one-off from Fraser. He could and should have been at Headingley and Lord's, so there is no room for selectorial smugness. When he also bowled Healy via the inside edge, he had taken two wickets for four runs from five overs yesterday and 2 for 30 in all from 19 overs. Compare that with Dilley's 0 for 80 from 18 overs, Jarvis's 0 for 61 from 15, and, for all the hype, Botham's 1 for 65 from 22, and a story emerges.

It was thanks to Dilley's benevolence that Jones was able to proceed so easily to his hundred. Three leg-stump half-volleys were dispatched with no more than a flick of the wrist, through square-leg for boundaries, the third of which took him to 97. He then lost Healy, but in the next over, Dilley obliged once more, this time short and wide. Jones swatted the ball to third man, ran this three, and raised arms and helmet in triumph. He is a very fine player.

Third Test, 3rd day

Australia 391–7

David Gower has no illusions about the tactics that England need to win the Test: bowl Australia out quickly on Monday, score 800 in four hours and put them under a bit of pressure. A piece of cake really.

It's typical Gower flippancy of course, and actually a tacit admission that there are only two results possible in the match and neither of them is an England win. With three days gone and – thanks to so much time lost to the weather – the Australian first innings not yet over, the odds must be on the draw. But it is not outside the realms of possibility that Australia could force the follow-on: if that happens, then with Alderman in his pomp England could be in trouble.

As it is, the chances of Gower retaining the Ashes are slipping elusively away. Those unprecedented consecutive Australian wins at Headingley and Lord's put them in such a position of strength that even with four matches to play, the odds were in their favour. Now, win or draw at Birmingham, they must be more so; to take two games out of three from a side performing so well, and, if they so desire, with the opportunity of playing exclusively not to lose, is, if not impossible, a pretty tall order.

The Third Test thus far has been a frustrating experience for England. At Headingley and Lord's they would have appreciated the intervention of the weather; but not here when every second counts. Instead, only 47 overs have been possible in two days.

On the third day, a low mizzle hung like muslin over the ground so that play could not begin until three o'clock. In two sessions, broken by a further 80-minute interruption for bad light and

drizzle, Australia, in 31 overs were able to extend their overnight 294 for 6 by a further 97 for the single loss of Merv Hughes, who, having batted so steadfastly in the first two Tests, ran out of steam and luck and was comfortably caught by Ian Botham at second slip in Graham Dilley's first over with only five more runs added to the total. But the eighth wicket stand between Dean Jones, who finished the day unbeaten on 141, and Trevor Hohns, whose 40 not out is comfortably the highest score of his Test career, has yielded 92 so far, helped by an unusual, if not unprecedented seven runs from one delivery which the bowler Dilley, who has already conceded far too many, was quick to establish were leg-byes.

These lower order partnerships are becoming a feature of the Australian innings. At Leeds, when they had lost 6 for 441, Steve Waugh and Hughes added 147, and at Lord's the last four wickets came close to doubling the total from 265 to 528, including a stand of 130 from Waugh and Geoff Lawson for the ninth wicket. There is no secret to it. Each time, a main batsman – Waugh at Leeds and Lord's, and now Jones at Edgbaston – has been involved. Rather than be given over to panic and a blaze of shots while the heavy roller is warmed up, Border has instructed these two batsmen to make sure that if they get out, they are the last to do so. He has then told the tail to sell their souls dearly. It has worked splendidly and with remarkably few hitches. Indeed at Lord's, Lawson, for example, played so well that not only was Waugh able to approach his second century of the series with circumspection, but he was able to have a breather afterwards.

The left-handed Hohns did an admirable job for Jones and Australia. With the atmosphere as heavy as it was, the pitch under cover for so long, and the light as dim – the batsmen did at one point actually refuse the chance to go off – it was certain that the ball would beat the bat more than it had done on the first day, and both Dilley and Angus Fraser obliged. But although Hughes edged an outswinger early on, and Hohns later, when 19, edged Jarvis pokily waist-high to second slip where Botham, apparently picking the ball up late against the dark background,

Scoreboard from Edgbaston

Australia

First Innings

		6s	4s	Mins	Balls
G R Marsh lbw Botham	42	–	2	145	134
M A Taylor st Russell b Emburey...	43	–	5	135	99
D C Boon run out (Jarvis)	38	–	5	134	111
*A R Border b Emburey	8	–	1	17	21
D M Jones not out	141	–	15	342	258
S R Waugh b Fraser	43	–	6	78	54
†I A Healy b Fraser	2	–	–	16	12
M G Hughes c Botham b Dilley......	2	–	–	19	16
T V Hohns not out	40	–	4	116	93
Extras (lb 20, nb 12)	32				
Total (7 wkts, 130 overs) _____	**391**				

G F Lawson and T M Alderman to bat.
FALL OF WICKETS: 1–88, 2–94, 3–105, 4–201, 5–272, 6–289, 7–299.
BOWLING: Dilley 25–2–103–1 (nb 15); Jarvis, 23–4–82–0; Fraser 27–7–50–2 (nb 3); Botham 26–5–75–1; Emburey 29–5–61–2.

dropped the chance, there was little to show for it. Jarvis needs a bit of success to give him confidence – he has thus far looked a nervous novice, which does not do his ability justice – but wouldn't you know, Hohns added insult to injury to driving the next ball for four. It can be a hard game.

Third Test, 4th day

Australia 424, England 185–7

It may have been the best of times and the worst of times two hundred years ago in Paris, but for English cricket, Birmingham, 1989, you can definitely delete the best. There have already been some depressingly low points this summer but when Kim Barnett edged a delivery from Steve Waugh to the keeper to reduce them to 75 for 5, England had reached a depth from which they would risk the bends if and when they ever bob to the surface again.

That they subsequently have come remotely close, after Australia were all out for 424, to reaching the 225 runs they need to save the follow-on and with it, given the lack of time left, the match, is entirely due to the good offices of Ian Botham, who is an old hand at retrieving lost causes, and Jack Russell who is rapidly learning the art. With Botham making 46 and Russell 42, they added 96 for the sixth wicket, before both fell in successive overs towards the end of the day. On the last morning, England will therefore require a further 40 with three wickets remaining, to make Australia bat again.

As England collapses go, this, on a decent enough pitch, was one out of the top drawer, a heady brew of poor technique, quality bowling – particularly, once more, from Terry Alderman, whose dismissal of Gower was the best piece of bowling of the series – and a pinch of stupidity. Of the first four wickets to fall, Gooch, Gower, and Curtis were all lbw, which meant that on 15 occasions England men had succumbed in that manner out of 45 dismissals; too high a percentage on good pitches.

Gooch is the most worrying as this was his fourth lbw in five Test innings. He has long had a tendency to plant his left leg early and work the ball to the on-side, which with bowlers often slanting the ball in to him from wide of the crease, doesn't generally find him wanting – the shot has brought him thousands of runs. Yesterday, after he and Curtis had added 17, it was Lawson's turn to expose it as a deficiency, when Gooch was caught half-forward and hitting all round a short ball that failed to bounce very high.

Gower, in a brave if mystifying move, given the situation and the presence of Tavaré, batted at three in place of Barnett who has strained not one but two groins. Alderman bowled brilliantly to him, snaking ball after ball past his flickering outside edge before, when the moment was absolutely right, applying the inswinging *coup de grâce*. The rueful look on Gower's face as he wandered off was that of a man who had known all along he would be done but was powerless to do anything about it.

With the end of Tavaré in Alderman's following over, a myth died. The old joke was that when the Mary Rose was raised from the Solent,

'This line-and-length business is so easy I could do it with my eyes closed' – *Angus Fraser at Edgbaston*

BELOW A helmeted Botham this time – but no less determined to carry the attack to Australia

ABOVE Another look at the historic dismissal of Steve Waugh – English supporters had to look twice to convince themselves that he really was out

Scoreboard from Edgbaston

Australia

First Innings

		6s	4s	Mins	Balls
G R Marsh lbw b Botham	42	–	2	145	134
M A Taylor st Russell b Emburey	43	–	5	135	99
D C Boon run out (Jarvis)	38	–	5	134	111
*A R Border b Emburey	8	–	1	17	21
D M Jones c sub (I Folley) b Fraser	157	–	17	327	293
S R Waugh b Fraser	43	–	6	78	54
†I A Healy b Fraser	2	–	–	16	12
M G Hughes c Botham b Dilley	2	–	–	19	16
T V Hohns c Gooch b Dilley	40	–	4	119	99
G F Lawson b Fraser	12	–	2	34	28
T M Alderman not out	0	–	–	9	8
Extras (lb 20, nb 17)	37				
Total (142 overs)	**424**				

FALL OF WICKETS: 1–88, 2–94, 3–105, 4–201, 5–272, 6–289, 7–299, 8–391, 9–421.
BOWLING: Dilley 31–3–123–2 (nb 17); Jarvis, 23–4–82–0; Fraser 33–8–63–4 (nb 6); Botham 26–5–75–1; Emburey 29–5–61–2.

England

First Innings

		6s	4s	Mins	Balls
G A Gooch lbw b Lawson	8	–	1	41	33
T S Curtis lbw b Hughes	41	–	7	121	81
*D I Gower lbw b Alderman	8	–	1	27	26
C J Tavaré c Taylor b Alderman	2	–	–	10	9
K J Barnett c Healy b Waugh	10	–	2	31	21
I T Botham b Hughes	46	–	6	154	110
†R C Russell c Taylor b Hohns	42	–	3	156	131
J E Emburey not out	2	–	–	28	21
A R C Fraser not out	12	–	1	22	24
Extras (b 1, lb 2, nb 11)	14				
Total (7 wkts, 74 overs)	**185**				

P W Jarvis and G R Dilley to bat.
FALL OF WICKETS: 1–17, 2–42, 3–47, 4–75, 5–75, 6–171, 7–171.
BOWLING: Alderman 21–6–45–2 (nb 5); Lawson 14–3–37–1; Waugh 11–3–38–1 (nb 6); Hughes 18–4–49–2 (nb 1); Hohns 10–4–13–1.

the way of all flesh, hitting around a straight ball. But the downfall of Barnett, batting with Gooch as a runner, was the most abject. In spite of his injury, or possibly – in that it restricted his initial movement – because of it, he played with admirable caution, striking one beautiful controlled off-side boundary in the process. Then suddenly, his brain appeared to go into overload. Twice he swished at Waugh and missed; he learned nothing, tried again, and this time, surely, edged himself out of the series.

Before Hughes beat Botham's drive and Hohns had Russell caught at slip as he aimed a cut, the pair had batted with commendable common sense. No Botham slog this: he pushed well forward, particularly to Alderman, used his pads with propriety and thumped half a dozen hearty boundaries. His dismissal, when in sight of his first half century of the season, was probably his first aberration.

Earlier, Australia had extended their first innings by 55 minutes and 33 runs, with Dean Jones last out for 157, the highest Test score on this ground by an Australian. He had batted for 6½ hours when he pulled a ball from Fraser to backward square leg. It was no less than Fraser deserved, and gave him debut figures of 33–8–63–4: under two runs per over and just four boundaries hit from him. He at least can be satisfied. As for the rest, Micky Stewart said that they do not think about defeat. Actually some of them don't seem to think very much at all.

Third Test, 5th day

Australia 424, and 158–2
England 242

As may confidently have been expected once the England tail had scraped and scrambled together the 40 runs required to make Australia bat again, the Third Test fizzled out to its inevitable drawn conclusion. The proceedings were brought to an end at 5.30 with Australia's second innings, little more than an afternoon's net practice, having

a survivor was discovered, whose first words were to enquire whether Tavaré had yet got off the mark. It took him only three balls yesterday – a squirt to third man – but it was all he got. Such frivolity deserves retribution; Alderman drew him forward and Taylor took the catch by his ankles at first slip.

Through all this, Curtis had looked in better order than most, cutting effectively when given the chance, but even he, after two hours, went reached 158 for 2, with Mark Taylor making 51, his third half century of the series in addition to his maiden Test century at Leeds. Earlier, England had finally been bowled out for 242, conceding a lead of 182.

It is a measure of the current expectation we have of the England team that when Paul Jarvis, more in desperation than anything, slogged Geoff Lawson back over the bowler's head for the boundary which saved England the ignominy of following on, it was as if they had actually lifted the Ashes, not merely reduced the first innings deficit to less than 200.

That England should, in a match that has lost ten hours' play to the weather, even get themselves into a position where they might lose is a serious indictment, although had they followed on, surely not even they would have been bowled out a second time on such a benign pitch.

When the post-mortem takes place, the position of every member of the side, except Fraser, Russell, and perhaps Emburey, because in his case there really is no alternative, ought to come under scrutiny. Since David Gower won the Ashes in 1985, England have now won just three games, including one against Sri Lanka last year, in the 37 Tests they have played, losing in that time as many games – 17 – as they have drawn. Put simply, they have been too bad for too long.

It is worth considering that in that period, the nucleus of the England side has consisted of players – Gower, Gatting, Gooch, Emburey, Botham, Dilley and Lamb – whose individual pedigree it is hard to call into question, but who have rarely been able to put together the collective performance, as Australia are now doing, that wins Tests. The time is getting close, if it hasn't already arrived, when a decision should be made as to whether this situation can be allowed to carry on any longer.

For example, when the team is selected for the Fourth Test at Old Trafford, there will certainly be at least one batting place – Barnett's – up for grabs and, if they are all fit and well, at least three candidates – Allan Lamb, Robin Smith and Mike Gatting – in the selectors' minds. The pecking order at present would probably read Lamb (aged 35), Gatting (32) and then Smith,

who is 10 years Lamb's junior; if they are looking to the future Smith should get the nod, but it's unlikely. Likewise, if England, as they may well do, decide that two spinners are necessary, and a seamer other than Jarvis has to go, they may well omit Fraser to make way for Foster, and retain Dilley. There is no reason why Botham's place should any longer be considered sacrosanct either. The fact that he made a relatively obdurate 46 in England's innings is scarcely earth-shattering except for the tabloids, and his bowling is a shadow of what it once was. Why should not David Capel be given an extended chance now?

England achieved their prime objective, scoring 225 runs, after 70 minutes batting in the morning, but they made heavy weather of it. The day began on a ridiculous note when, with quite literally all day to bat if necessary, Fraser pushed the fifth ball from Hohns square on the off side, and set off for a single that was a figment of his imagination alone. Even a fielder as cumbersome as Hughes had time to pounce, and throw to the keeper before Fraser, sent back by Emburey, was even within earshot. Emburey and Dilley then set about things in a more responsible manner, with Dilley defending resolutely while Emburey selectively blocked everything unless it was short and wide, and collected the runs, mostly in boundaries.

Border was able to take the new ball – the crux of the day – after the first 11 overs had yielded 24 runs and 18 were still required, and immediately Emburey, on 24, was missed by Marsh in the gully off Lawson. It was an important moment, for the pair were able to eke out a further half a dozen runs before Emburey attempted to pull a short ball from Lawson and mistimed a simple catch to mid-on.

Dilley meanwhile, for all his fortitude, can consider himself lucky to have survived a couple of lbw appeals off Alderman that looked remarkably adjacent. With just the one wicket remaining, and 10 still to get, there appeared to be a conflict of approaches between Dilley ('we can get 'em in singles') and Jarvis ('with overthrows, I can probably get 'em in one hit'). That his way succeeded was like putting all your roulette chips on red and seeing it come up. It might just as

Scoreboard from Edgbaston

Australia

First innings: 424 (D M Jones 157; A R C Fraser 4 for 63).

Second Innings

	6s	4s	Mins	Balls
M A Taylor c Botham b Gooch 51	–	4	172	148
G R Marsh b Jarvis 42	–	4	111	86
D C Boon not out 22	–	1	116	112
†I E Healy not out 33	–	3	55	46
Extras (b 4, lbw 4, nb 2)........... 10				
Total (2 wkts, 65 overs)_____ 158				

*A R Border, D M Jones, S R Waugh, T V Hohns, M G Hughes, G F Lawson and T M Alderman did not bat.
FALL OF WICKETS: 1–81, 2–109.
BOWLING: Dilley 10–4–27–0; Fraser 12–0–29–0 (nb 2); Embury 20–8–37–0; Jarvis 6–1–20–1; Gooch 14–5–31–1; Curtis 3–0–6–0.

England

First Innings

	6s	4s	Mins	Balls
G A Gooch lbw b Lawson 8	–	1	41	33
T S Curtis lbw b Hughes................ 41	–	7	121	81
*D I Gower lbw b Alderman 8	–	1	27	26
C J Tavaré c Taylor b Alderman 2	–	–	10	9
K J Barnett c Healy b Waugh.......... 10	–	2	31	21
I T Botham b Hughes 46	–	6	154	110
†R C Russell c Taylor b Hohns....... 42	–	3	156	13
J E Embury c Boon b Lawson 26	–	5	76	58
A R C Fraser run out (Hughes–				
Healy) 12	–	1	24	29
G R Dilley not out 11	–	1	85	63
P W Jarvis lbw b Alderman 22	–	2	39	31
Extras (b 1, lb 2, nb 11)............... 14				
Total (96.3 overs) _____ 242				

FALL OF WICKETS: 1–17, 2–42, 3–47, 4–75, 5–75, 6–171, 7–171, 8–185, 9–215.
BOWLING: Alderman 26.3–6–61–3 (nb 5); Lawson 21–4–54–2; Waugh 11–3–38–1 (nb 6); Hughes 22–4–68–2 (nb 2); Hohns 16–8–18–1.

Man of the match: D M Jones.

easily have been black, and one hopes the outcome is not viewed as a triumph.

Postscript

Australians will be hoping that when a bolt of lightning struck their national flag from its mast, during the ferocious tropical storm that closed the first day's play, it was not someone trying to tell them something. Were it not for the loss of ten hours' playing time to the elements, Australia would almost certainly – you can never be absolutely certain in this game – have beaten England's raggle-taggle band for the third time in a row; and that, in terms of the Ashes, would have been that. But the Mother of Fortune is smiling her quirky smile. Not yet boys, not yet, she tells the Aussies. It's going too well for you; too cocky by half. A bit more sweating to do yet.

Certainly the weather has given England hope where at first it heralded despair. England needed a good result at Edgbaston not only to remain in contention for the series, but to restore some credibility: their performances had fast become a national joke. Thursday night's rain was viewed at the time as a major setback, but by the time the sun returned to duty, its blessings were obvious to all.

Once more the Australian bowling exposed faulty English techniques, gorged on the junk-food necessities of one-day cricket. Gooch has problems at present, not helped by Border's merciless tourniquet of a field, but he surely is good enough to work them out; time is running out for him, though. Gower was assassinated: a hapless victim of thought, planning and execution. The rest could have learned from Botham, who was the only English batsman to show solid basics. His innings of 46, in any other era, would have been disregarded as humble run-of-the-mill fare. But here it shone like a beacon in a stormy sea of incompetence.

Australia's batsmen, by contrast, continue to give batting lessons. This time, with the unexpected departure of Steve Waugh, who at least has rejoined the human race by acquiring an average, it was Professor Jones who held the podium. He is a trim, prancing thoroughbred all right, who knows he has talent and so obviously revels in parading it. When he reached his century, he saluted his team mates in the pavilion, as is the modern vogue. But not before he had acknowledged the applause from all corners of the ground. It was the gesture of a man who knows his role: great actors no doubt accept the plaudits of their peers, but they take their curtain calls first. It is a small point, but it means a great deal to the public, who are sometimes made to feel as if they are an incidental to the proceedings.

Ominously, this series has yet to see a major innings from either Geoff Marsh or Allan Border. If they were English, you would assume it was loss of form, confidence or whatever, but for them it seems to be just part of the process. There is, you get the feeling, no point in everyone peaking at the same time. Border and Marsh will make their presence before too long.

For the moment, Australia are on a magnificent run. The confidence oozes sweetly in everything they do, from the strutting warm-up run to the micrometer-precise field placings that show how little of the time that Allan Border and Terry Alderman have spent in county cricket has been wasted. It has put English planning, clod-hopping by comparison, to shame.

Yet there is a danger – and not just to Australia – in England surviving with a draw. Should they now sneak a win at Old Trafford – perfectly feasible if only because Alderman could so easily break down – it would leave them with only one to win from two remaining games to square the series and retain the Ashes. The consequences of them doing this are too disastrous to contemplate, and it is not being unpatriotic to suggest it. For if they succeed at Old Trafford it will be with the old guard, who would then retain their places for the rest of the series. The end, we would be told, would justify the means. Not so: no wins now, however worthy they might be, could erase the humiliating displays thus far. The selectors shirked blooding Angus Fraser until it was too late; don't think they can stop there.

Fourth Cornhill Test Match

England v Australia, Old Trafford, 27 July–1 August 1989

Match Preview

What, one wonders, is actually going through the minds of England's cricketers as they face up to the Fourth Test at Old Trafford? Outwardly, it is clear cut: if they lose, then it's goodbye Ashes; draw and there is still a glimmer; win and who knows what might happen.

But the mental side is no different from any other game. The Australians, reaping the benefit of the togetherness that touring brings, have reached an inner strength that England, gathering together only on the afternoon before, have as yet been unable to approach. Winning – or losing as the case may be – plays its part too in perpetuating the state of affairs. Success, as the cliché says, breeds more of the same. So when the English think-tank of Gower, Dexter and Stewart collectively convey the notion that the England team has never been more determined than it is now, you have to believe them. But they, as the lady opined, they would say that wouldn't they.

Inwardly it must be different. Quite simply, it becomes increasingly hard to motivate and be motivated when things continually fail to go your way, and that is how England have fared in this series so far. The general air of abstraction cannot be helped by the uncertainty surrounding the future – South African or otherwise – of some of England's leading players, and with things like that on the minds of players, it is impossible, whatever they might say, for them to concentrate one hundred per cent on the job in hand. One press colleague suggested that he had seen a similar atmosphere surrounding the pre-Packer Australians, and Dexter is aware of the damage that can be done. 'It is clearly unsatisfactory,' was his view on the eve of this Test Match, 'that another cricketing promoter outside standard international Test cricket is in the business of committing some of our players.'

The implication was, though, that if some of those players to whom Dexter and Gower have remained loyal don't come up with the goods, and England lose here, then that could mean cards and money in any case. 'If we go 3–0 down, and have therefore lost the Ashes,' said Dexter, 'then selection for the remaining two Tests would be in a different light. I expect David Gower to play a very important part in that process.'

This last part is a riposte to a story that appeared in a Sunday tabloid, in which it was suggested that Gower would resign if the Ashes were lost. All Gower would say was that he would 'consider his position' in the unlikely event of England losing again.

Plans to avoid this have been thwarted once more by injuries to key players; and to their number can be added, yet again, Graham Dilley, whose suspect knee flared up. He spent Wednesday afternoon at a Manchester hospital with a consultant rather than at practice and is less than likely to play; Paul Jarvis has been called into the squad as cover. Whether England include him in their final side, or opt to play two spinners, John Emburey and Nick Cook, will not be decided until Thursday morning, but the vibes from Peter Marron, the groundsman, are that the pitch – a re-laid one, hitherto unused – will turn. 'It was last watered eight days ago,' said Marron on Wednesday, 'and there are cracks in it.'

Australia could take a similar view on selection. They would like to play the side that has served them so well, but if Tim May comes into the reckoning, then it will be in addition to, rather than at the expense of Trevor Hohns, and Merv Hughes could be the one to go.

Fourth Test, 1st Day

England 224–7

England's batsmen, already sitting in the selectorial equivalent of Death Row, could not have gone much further towards giving Allan Border a present of the Ashes on his birthday if they'd gift-wrapped the urn, stuck 34 candles on it and sung 'For He's a Jolly Good Fellow'.

That England are still in with a shout in this Test, even after batting first on a pitch hard and dry as a ship's biscuit and already showing signs of turn, is due entirely to a marvellous maiden Test century from Robin Smith, who has made an unbeaten 112; an innings full of skill, determination and good old-fashioned bottle, qualities not much evident in many other English batsmen so far this series.

Ken Barrington, who made 254 against Australia on this ground a quarter of a century ago, used to play such flag-flying knocks, and he surely beamed a grin of approval from above.

But what he would have said about the rest of the batting would not bear repeating. Earlier this summer, England tried the blitzkreig approach, with notable lack of success. Today, for a while, as an antidote, they tried catatonic inactivity – in one 66-minute spell before lunch the scoreboard creaked up a measly two singles – in an effort to bore Australia into submission. That didn't work either.

They even resorted to an up-and-at-'em visit at lunchtime from a naval helicopter pilot, in the form of Prince Andrew, to up spirits, which worked for a while, but in the end there is no substitute for application and technique allied. 224 for 7 represents perhaps three wickets too many in normal circumstances; in view of what had preceded it, it can be seen instead as a minor triumph.

The Australians once again demonstrated their uncompromising, thoughtful cricket and a capacity, in the interests of team spirit it almost appears, for spreading the glory. It would be unreasonable to expect Terry Alderman to do it time after time, so the spotlight switched instead to Geoff Lawson and Trevor Hohns, who shared all the English wickets. Lawson, gliding leggily in for over after over – 27 in all – was something like the performer of old, producing his best bowling of the series. He's short of pace now, but his timing and wristiness produced enough skiddy inswing to make life distinctly awkward for the English batsmen. The contrast was provided by the leg-spin of Hohns, whom Border had whirling away by half-past midday, usually time sacred to the god of seam on the first morning. Until some late lustiness from Foster spoiled his figures, he had toiled splendidly.

But well as they bowled and as cunningly as Border schemed, an England slump to 158 for 7, having won a good toss, can only be ascribed once more to woeful batting. All the wickets to fall were either bowled or lbw, which on a good pitch tells a sorry story of yet more bad strokes and poor concentration.

The start belied the day, as Gooch and Curtis, surviving three raucous lbw shouts from Alderman, tucked away 23 runs in the first eight overs. Things for once looked rosy, and the crowd purred with the anticipation of good things to

Smith acknowledges the Old Trafford crowd after reaching his hundred in the Fourth Test

ABOVE It pays to attack: Smith in full flow

BELOW But there again ... Botham takes a swing at Hohns' leg-spin and is bowled for 0

Scoreboard from Old Trafford

England won toss

England

First Innings

		6s	4s	Mins	Balls
G A Gooch b Lawson	11	–	1	50	32
T S Curtis b Lawson	22	–	4	136	103
R T Robinson lbw b Lawson	0	–	–	15	9
R A Smith not out	112	–	12	295	237
*D I Gower lbw b Hohns	35	–	6	86	51
I T Botham b Hohns	0	–	–	7	6
†R C Russell lbw b Lawson	1	–	–	12	11
J E Emburey lbw b Hohns	5	–	1	38	34
N A Foster not out	36	1	4	75	57
Extras (lb 2)	2				
Total (7 wkts, 90 overs)	**224**				

A R C Fraser and N G B Cook to bat.
FALL OF WICKETS: 1–23, 2–23, 3–57, 4–132, 5–140, 6–147, 7–158.
BOWLING: Alderman 20–12–35–0; Lawson 27–9–58–4; Hughes 15–6–47–0; Hohns 22–7–59–3; Waugh 6–1–23–0.

Australia

G R Marsh, M A Taylor, D C Boon, *A R Border, D M Jones, S R Waugh, †I A Healy, M G Hughes, T V Hohns, G F Lawson and T M Alderman.

Umpires: B J Meyer and J H Hampshire.

come. Instead the innings went to sleep and Lawson plucked out its heart. Before Smith and David Gower administered the kiss of life with a stand of 75, Gooch had been bowled, the ball flicking the top of his pad; Robinson, dozy as if not quite out of hibernation, was lbw for nought; and Curtis, after more than two hours' studious occupation of the crease for 22, was let down by his technique, hitting across the line.

For an hour or so, Gower and Smith batted as comfortably as any English pair had this summer, with the captain wistful and delicate, and his ally belligerent, straight in defence, and defiant and positive in attack. Together they could and should have put England into the comfort zone. Instead, Gower heaved an inelegant pull at a quicker ball from Hohns that hurried on and kept low, and was lbw. Nor was there a miracle from Ian Botham. In Hohns' next over, the red mist rose, he rampaged down the pitch, slogged horrendously and was bowled. He

marched off clutching his head as if to check there was a brain in there. As he did so, the royal standard was struck from the pavilion mast, and a helicopter whirred away. One was orf; there is, it seemed to say, only so much a chap can do.

But if that was the worst moment of a bad summer, it was surpassed in no time at all. After Russell became another Lawson victim immediately after tea, Emburey partnered Smith for 40 untroubled minutes before swatting gently across the line, a stroke whose stupefying ineptness will take some matching.

Quite how Smith felt about all this is hard to tell. Probably it served to make him even more determined. He had already passed 50 with Gower at the crease, had made 84 by the time Emburey was out, and was in danger of running out of partners. But Foster, not without a slice of luck, kept him company for the last hour and a quarter, in an eighth-wicket stand that has so far produced 66 runs, during which Smith, after four and a quarter hours at the crease, forced Alderman through extra cover for the four that took him to his hundred. That perhaps, at last, is the beginning of the new era.

Fourth Test, 2nd Day

England 260
Australia 219–3

Here continueth the fourth lesson. Just as almost every day so far in the series has gone to Australia, so today belonged almost totally to Allan Border and his men. England, who had begun the second day on 224 for 7, managed to prolong things for the best part of an hour against the new ball, and when Robin Smith, 112 overnight, was last out for 143, they had reached 260, a total, the pundits felt, that might make Australia struggle.

Not a bit of it. On the stroke of six o'clock, Border was able to poddle contentedly off the field with 219 on the board, only three Australian wickets down, Dean Jones one short of a half-century, and himself, ominously in view of his relatively poor personal series, on a very determined 19, chiselled out of 30 overs. He, you can bet, is out to make an impact of his own.

The only hiccup to another thorough hiding came in a 12-over spell either side of tea, when England not only finally broke the opening partnership, at 135 by some distance the highest and easiest of the series, by dismissing Geoff Marsh for 47, but then went on and captured the further wickets of his opening partner Mark Taylor for 85 and, for good measure, that of David Boon for 12, all for the addition of 19 runs. It might have heralded the start of a brave comeback by England, but unfortunately it didn't. Border, grafting nugget that he is, and Jones, as busy as a high street Saturday with six fours and a six already, have added 65 for the fourth wicket to take Australia within 42 runs of yet another first innings lead.

From an English viewpoint it made sorry watching. Before the match, Micky Stewart had assured us that the will to win in the England dressing room was as great as it was when last England retained the Ashes. For determination in the dressing room there is not a side to touch them. A pity, then, that it is not more obvious on the field. Australia are buzzing, and with good reason. It is easy to do, of course, when you are utterly in charge; there is every right to strut. But they look competitive, Border's field placings are positively claustrophobic – there are times when it is necessary to count the fielders to make sure he hasn't slipped a couple extra on – and the bowlers receive superb backing from them. They in turn respond; it is the musketeer spirit of all for one and one for all. England by contrast looked shambling, disorganised, adrift (preoccupied?). Shoulders hunch, arms are folded, they slope around between overs. There is no spark any more; good players, fine players some of them, appear to have nothing left to give.

The Marsh–Taylor stand was further evidence of the planning that Border and Bobby Simpson have put into the tour. There were those, myself included, who were astounded that they should wish to break up the prolific partnership that

Marsh had forged with David Boon. Now no one can doubt the wisdom and Taylor, a left-handed counterpoint to Marsh, has been one of the outstanding successes of the series, with previous scores of 136, 60, 62, 27, 43, 51, and now 85 more: 464 in all.

Things were made easier than they might have been for the openers by first of all, some lacklustre new-ball bowling – Foster and Fraser both bowled too short – and later, a general lack of response for the spinners. And Ian Botham, who might have been expected to feature somewhere, for some reason didn't even enter into the equation until the 37th over when the score had topped the hundred, which, since he was the only other seamer, was mystifying. Injured, perhaps? Apparently not. Instead it was another bit of Gower instinct. The pitch it was suggested, did not suit him, but given that Alderman had swung the ball earlier (they are using the controversial 'Reader' incidentally, the sort with a seam like a ship's hawser, which England won the right to use on the toss of a coin), that it was overcast, and that the Ashes were slipping away, it might have been worth a punt from the miracle worker. When he did appear, it was in the middle of a madcap period that saw the ball beating a tattoo on the boundary boards and 34 runs in four overs. His first over, bowled like a rusty door opening, produced 13 runs; his fourth and penultimate typically brought the breakthrough. Marsh went to glance, and Russell, standing up to the stumps, took a superb catch down the leg side. He at least can look back on the s..ies with some pride.

Russell had a glove in the second dismissal as well, when Emburey, just as he did at Edgbaston, lured Taylor down the pitch and spun it past his outside edge. Taylor will have to learn that playing with the likes of Alderman has its plusses but rough created outside the left-hander's off-stump is not one of them. Five overs later Boon had gone, Gattinged with bat in the air by Fraser, who bowled with more purpose after tea.

Earlier, Geoff Lawson had helped to remove the remaining three English wickets, to finish with figures of 6 for 72. The first, Foster, was caught at the second attempt by Border at short extra cover as the batsman drove, and the

Scoreboard from Old Trafford

England

First Innings

	6s	4s	Mins	Balls
G A Gooch b Lawson	11	–	1	50	32
T S Curtis b Lawson	22	–	4	136	103
R T Robinson lbw b Lawson............	0	–	–	15	9
R A Smith c Hohns b Hughes	143	–	15	355	285
*D I Gower lbw b Hohns	35	–	6	86	51
I T Botham b Hohns	0	–	–	7	6
†R C Russell lbw b Lawson.............	1	–	–	12	11
J E Emburey lbw b Hohns	5	–	1	38	34
N A Foster c Border b Lawson	39	1	4	100	68
A R C Fraser lbw b Lawson	2	–	–	16	9
N G B Cook not out	0	–	–	15	10
Extras (lb 2)	2				
Total (103 overs)	**260**				

FALL OF WICKETS: 1–23, 2–23, 3–57, 4–132, 5–140, 6–147, 7–158, 8–232, 9–252.
BOWLING: Alderman 25–13–49–0; Lawson 33–11–72–6; Hughes 17–6–55–1; Hohns 22–7–59–3; Waugh 6–1–23–0.

Australia

First Innings

	6s	4s	Mins	Balls
M A Taylor st Russell b Emburey...	85	–	10	179	180
G R Marsh c Russell b Botham.......	47	–	5	158	100
D C Boon b Fraser	12	–	2	40	40
*A R Border not out	19	–	1	107	88
D M Jones not out	49	1	6	88	77
Extras (b 1, lb 3, nb 3).................	7				
Total (3 wkts, 80 overs)	**219**				

S R Waugh, †I A Healy, M G Hughes, T V Hohns, G F Lawson and T M Alderman to bat.

FALL OF WICKETS: 1–135, 2–143, 3–154.
BOWLING: Foster 17–8–35–0; Fraser 22–3–60–1 (nb 5); Emburey 23–6–69–1; Cook 13–4–36–0; Botham 5–2–15–1.

second, Fraser, was another lbw victim. But they kept Smith company long enough for him to hit another three boundaries, including one thunderous off-drive, before he upper-cut a bouncer from Hughes and was well caught by Hohns at third man. For the future of English cricket, his six hours at the crease had been time well spent.

Fourth Test, 3rd Day

England 260
Australia 441–9

The Ashes are just about in Australian hands again. On the first day of this Fourth Test, England, Robin Smith a glorious exception, failed with the bat and on the second they failed with the ball. So when the third day began, with Australia ˜a mere 41 runs behind with seven wickets in hand and the pitch looking as good as any this summer, it really looked a question, barring intervention from the weather, of how long Border chose to prolong the game before accepting immortality.

Well, the day was shortened by 55 minutes, and sure enough Australia batted right through, taking their score from 219 to 441. But in the process of building their 181 run lead, they have lost nine of their wickets, five of them for 79 runs at the end of the day when England, on the ropes and close to being counted out to avoid further punishment, found the last dregs of spirit and gained some reward. The prognosis is still not good. No matter how good a pitch is, the mere fact that you are a couple of hundred runs away from even making the opposition bat again places mental pressures over and above the norm, and England will have to bat their skins off to remain in the series.

Previous Australia first-innings totals in this series of 601, 528 and 424 have been fundamental to their success, indicating an aptitude to work single-mindedly towards a goal. Saturday's effort was in keeping with that philosophy. In this case, with the bleached, biscuity pitch sure to deteriorate later, a substantial first innings lead was even more the order of the day; runs in the bank now would probably be worth double, batting last. Not one of the main batsmen let the cause down, although Smith remains the only centurion in the match so far.

If ever a century could be squeezed out by sheer will-power, it seemed certain that Border, heading for his finest hour, would do so. He has two hundreds, both made in adversity, in 1981 and 1985, to his credit on this ground and he grafted and concentrated so hard for more than five hours in pursuit of another you could have exploded a grenade behind him and he wouldn't have noticed. Tiredness ultimately did for him. And it seemed odds on that Dean Jones, 49 not out overnight and whose hyperactive work-rate is such that his bat must be of willow with E additives, would add another hundred to his outstanding 157 at Edgbaston. It was not to be.

You don't get realistic odds on Steve Waugh making a century, and yet again he was a marvel of sheer undiluted, uncomplicated talent and a timeless reminder of how the game should be played. Border was asked earlier this season whether he had plans to move Waugh up the batting order from six. 'Why?' he replied 'Isn't he doing well enough where he is?' This summer, there are already 485 reasons why he should stay where he is for the time being. But not even he could reach three figures this time.

Yet it wasn't until the last session that England remotely shook off some of the languor that has hovered over them all series, and bit back. By tea, just one Australian wicket had fallen in close on three sessions play: that of Jones who succumbed to the English disease and hit across his pad to be bowled by Botham. The bowling had been ragged at first, it was tidy at times later, but on the whole uncompetitive. The batsmen looked in no danger of getting out, content as they were to play good balls on merit and wait for the inevitable gift. After tea though, Foster at last found fire in his belly and removed Border to a low catch at the wicket, albeit via a tired, weak dab. Healy then paid the penalty of Foster's resultant adrenalin flow and was lbw next ball.

It inspired England to perhaps their best session in the field of the series. Suddenly the fielding, led by Smith, was alert and purposeful, and it paid dividends. Hohns, after adding 51 with Waugh, edged Cook onto his pad and into Gower's midriff at silly mid-off, and Hughes played an appalling stroke to a ball that deserved nothing less than a boundary. But the prize wicket was that of Waugh. Nothing, in a summer

of inevitabilities, was more so than his third hundred of the series. Instead, with only eight more needed, Fraser banged in a bouncer and Waugh, surprised perhaps, pulled hastily, failed to keep the shot down and Curtis, jumping at square leg, pulled down a memorable catch from above his head.

After play, another issue arose when David Gower, after consultation with Ted Dexter and the TCCB media representative, opted out of the traditional mid-Test meeting with the media. I can't say now that I blame him.

It follows on the heels of his walk-out on the corresponding day of the Lord's Test. At that time, it was suggested that it had been prompted by supposedly aggressive querying of his tactics by former players. Gower has since privately and publicly, in print, apologised to me for conveying this impression, and the truth lay elsewhere in the pages of the tabloids.

Now cricket writing, as far as possible, ought to involve one's own judgement without resort to the players' opinions to provide the meat. Unfortunately, tabloid sensationalism and the endless demand for 'quotes' – often tickled up in the office – has changed the thinking. A quote acts as a camouflage for lack of knowledge and an easy life whereby an 'angle' is handed on plate, and quite simply, the tabloids could not work without them – hence the demand for press conferences. The TCCB, unwisely, have acceded to this and have reaped the whirlwind. So when Gower took on the job of captain, he also agreed, rightly or wrongly, that he would conduct three conferences per Test – at the start, midway and at the end.

Sportsmen are very good at accepting praise but less so at taking criticism, so when he walked out at Lord's, I was of the opinion that it was his duty to have honoured the terms of his employment and that just because he had not enjoyed the best of days was no excuse. Now I'm not so sure. Because questions about cricket are a rarity at these gatherings – one really does try to make up one's own mind and stand or fall by that – the mid-Test conferences in particular tend to wallow in a mire of triviality. 'Do you think you can save the Test, David? . . . Will you resign,

Scoreboard from Old Trafford

England

First Innings: 260 (R A Smith 143; G F Lawson 6 for 72).

Australia

First Innings

	6s	4s	Mins	Balls
M A Taylor st Russell b Emburey...	85	–	10	179	180
G R Marsh c Russell b Botham.......	47	–	5	156	100
D C Boon b Fraser	12	–	2	40	40
*A R Border c Russell b Foster.......	80	–	10	312	266
D M Jones b Botham......................	69	1	7	173	141
S R Waugh c Curtis b Fraser...........	92	–	7	203	174
†I A Healy lbw b Foster	0	–	–	1	1
T V Hohns c Gower b Cook...........	17	–	2	62	64
M G Hughes b Cook	3	–	–	9	6
G F Lawson not out	13	–	2	23	23
T M Alderman not out	5	–	–	16	9
Extras (b 5, lb 6, w 1, nb 6).........	18				
Total (9 wkts, 166 overs)	**441**				

FALL OF WICKETS: 1–135, 2–143, 3–154, 4–274, 5–362, 6–362, 7–413, 8–423, 9–423.

BOWLING: Foster 33–12–69–2; Fraser 36–4–95–2 (nb 8); Emburey 45–9–118–1; Cook 28–6–85–2; Botham 24–6–63–2 (w 1).

David? ... Are you going to South Africa, David?'

And Gower, bless him, usually manages to convey the impression through gritted teeth that it's looking increasingly hard but yes, of course we can save it if Angus Fraser gets his first double hundred and Both takes 10 for 1. It is his nature to be communicative and provide the tabloids with their 'line', but the sheer banality of the conferences drives him, and many of the participants, to distraction and makes them unworkable.

So, after England had suffered another bad day, there arose a paradox: Micky Stewart, the England team manager, fielded things on his own and the business became suddenly quotable because of Gower's absence. 'In the light of the continued attacks David has had, both personal and in some cases abusive, it was felt it would not be the most productive move to have him here this evening,' said Stewart. This is a direct reference to the sort of tale that magnifies the mouthing of a single pavilion drunk into a major lobby. Win, lose or draw, Gower intends to be there on Tuesday evening post-match, and that is how it should be.

Gower has had a poor series – out-played and out-manœuvred – and he deserves to be criticised for that as much as he would have been praised had the situation been reversed. But to have his character continually and increasingly assassinated is another thing altogether. There are perhaps those who lie down with the wolves by taking large payments for ghosted columns. There are those, too, who are happily wined and dined one minute and then grumble when they are subsequently misquoted or taken out of context. They deserve what they get, or at least have less cause to complain. But it must be better if the captain and indeed the players, now and in the future, are kept out of the way until the job is done.

Fourth Test, 4th Day

England 260 and 123–6
Australia 447

By the end of the fourth day, the terminally sick soul that is English cricket was still clinging desperately to life by the slenderest of threads. Serious damage to the English second innings, but above all to any remaining semblance of pride, was sustained during a period of play as depressing to watch as any since perhaps England were humiliated by West Indies on this ground a year ago, and there have been quite a few bad moments since then. For in a spell of 23 overs, they lost every single one of their six main batsmen, Gooch, Curtis, Robinson, Smith, Gower and Botham for 59 runs.

In the end, only an unbroken seventh-wicket stand of 64 between the young Jack Russell terrier and the old dog John Emburey, followed by heavy spearing rain, saved England from the ultimate embarrassment of not only losing but doing so well inside four days, at one and the same time meekly handing over the Ashes to Allan Border.

England had taken less than two overs of the morning session to terminate the Australian first innings, 441 overnight, for the addition of just six more runs, which left them needing 187 to avoid an innings defeat. There was little chance that, battered and bruised, they could manœuvre themselves from a position as precarious as theirs into a physical and mental state whereby they could even remotely entertain the thought of winning, this in spite of the possibility that the pitch could deteriorate and make batting last a hazardous business. But with application, guts, determination, and, not least, a bit of luck, it could be saved. Problems start though when the opposition themselves possess not only these qualities in abundance, but can also add a massive, unshakeable self-confidence.

It was Border's old warriors Terry Alderman and the hero of the England first innings Geoff Lawson, both pampered and cossetted through this tour, who produced the goods when it really mattered. Between them they removed, with surgical precision the last trace of self-esteem left in the England team.

Fleetingly, very fleetingly, it had seemed that the counter-punch was there. Gooch ran Lawson's first ball to the third-man boundary and clumped the third contemptuously square for another; ten runs in all from that first over. What followed was a sorry procession of players who horrifyingly knew what they were perpetrating and what the implications were, but were as powerless as rabbits in the headlights to do anything about it.

Alderman, astonishingly, had failed to take a wicket in the first innings, and it must have rankled. He didn't have to wait long. Curtis survived a close yell for lbw first ball, but to the second he played forward, edged thinly onto his pad and Boon snaffled the chance at short leg. Robinson survived for seven overs, and then began a chain of three wickets in as many overs. In the first innings he had been dismissed without scoring, stepping onto his back foot, squaring up to Lawson and being lbw. Ditto yesterday – 27 for 2. In the following over from Alderman, Robin Smith, who has been one of the three outstanding England players in this abject summer – add to that list Russell and Angus Fraser – and who had made a marvellous century in the first innings, flicked down the leg side and Healy moved across for the catch. 27 for 3 and the worst England start of the summer.

Nor was it long before the error was compounded. This time it was Gooch who in Lawson's next over, with only a single added, was drawn into a forward stroke, only to see the ball jag away towards first slip where Alderman delightedly picked up the catch at daisy height. Not even Gower, trying so hard to squeeze every drop of experience from a weary mind, could arrest the slide. Nor could Botham, who stormed onto the field, bat swinging as of old, mane unconfined by a helmet. That lion though must sadly have roared his last, for Alderman straightened one up just enough to satisfy the umpire.

It now became a question of milestones, or probably at this end of the market, of millstones being passed. A Gower off-drive took England to 47, past the lowest ever total against Australia, and a three punched by Russell off the back foot, which brought up the 50, equalled their lowest in this country. It also took the England total aggregate in the match to 312, one more than the Australian team manager, Bobby Simpson, managed in one innings here in 1964. But Gower ran out of luck, for after 67 minutes he cut Lawson hard to gully and Marsh, who has not enjoyed the best of series there, clung on. At 59 for 6 it looked like the champagne could go on ice.

Russell and Emburey made sure it could remain so until the final day. With an admirable mixture of untroubled defence, canny nudging (from Emburey, who else?) and some authentic quality strokes (from Russell, who else?), the scoreboard ticked up. Past 71, their lowest on this ground . . . past 93, wiping out the horror of last year . . . and past 95, the lowest on the ground against Australia. Only once did they look troubled, when, with tea and the rain imminent, Russell offered no stroke to Border, who with the light failing had brought himself on, as he spun one out of the rough. But umpire Barrie Meyer, to Border's disgust, was unimpressed.

The end may come soon. The forecast will not

ABOVE Always plotting and scheming – Border's captaincy throughout the series was inspired

RIGHT Border congratulates Russell on his first ever century in first-class cricket. The England keeper went on to make an undefeated 128

Lawson appeals from a sitting position

Boon salutes his team-mates (LEFT) after hitting the runs that clinched the Fourth Test, the series and the Ashes, and (RIGHT) celebrates the victory with Mark Taylor

Scoreboard from Old Trafford

England

First Innings: 260 (R A Smith 143; G F Lawson 6 for 72).

Second Innings

	6s	4s	Mins	Balls
G A Gooch c Alderman b Lawson..	13	–	2	51	23
T S Curtis c Boon b Alderman	0	–	–	6	2
R T Robinson lbw b Lawson...........	12	–	1	31	28
R A Smith c Healy b Alderman.......	1	–	–	5	8
*D I Gower c Marsh b Lawson.......	15	–	1	67	40
I T Botham lbw b Alderman............	4	–	–	24	23
†R C Russell not out	47	–	6	120	109
J E Emburey not out	23	–	5	82	71
Extras (lb 3, w 2, nb 3).................	8				
Total (6 wkts, 50 overs)	**123**				

A R C Fraser, N A Foster and N G B Cook to bat.
FALL OF WICKETS: 1–10, 2–25, 3–27, 4–28, 5–38, 6–59.
BOWLING: Lawson 17–4–46–3; Alderman 13–1–38–3; Hohns 12–8–11–0; Hughes 5–0–22–0; Border 3–1–3–0.

Australia

First Innings

	6s	4s	Mins	Balls
M A Taylor st Russell b Emburey...	85	–	10	179	180
G R Marsh c Russell b Botham.......	47	–	5	156	100
D C Boon b Fraser	12	–	2	40	40
*A R Border c Russell b Foster.......	80	–	10	312	266
D M Jones b Botham	69	1	7	173	141
S R Waugh c Curtis b Fraser...........	92	–	7	203	174
†I A Healy lbw b Foster	0	–	–	1	1
T V Hohns c Gower b Cook............	17	–	2	62	64
M G Hughes b Cook	3	–	–	9	6
G F Lawson b Fraser	17	–	3	29	31
T M Alderman not out	6	–	–	22	12
Extras (b 5, lb 7, w 1, nb 6).........	19				
Total (167.5 overs)	**447**				

FALL OF WICKETS: 1–135, 2–143, 3–154, 4–274, 5–362, 6–362, 7–413, 8–423, 9–423.
BOWLING: Foster 34–12–74–2; Fraser 36.5–4–95–3 (nb 8); Emburey 45–9–118–1; Cook 28–6–85–2; Botham 24–6–83–2 (w 1).

allow for the weather to deprive Border and Australia, nor would it be worthy if it did. Border, who has trodden the rocky path England now tread, deserves his glory.

Fourth Test, 5th Day

England 260 and 264
Australia 447 and 81–1
Australia won by 9 wickets

At twenty to six on a breezy, sunny Cowes of an afternoon, David Boon, as chunky a symbol of Aussie defiance as ever walked an English Test pitch, swept Nick Cook to the square-leg boundary, and pandemonium broke out. It took Australia, in their second innings, to 81 giving them victory over England by 9 wickets – their third win of the series and their 100th in all – and with it the Ashes.

Allan Border, a man who as captain and player has seen enough of the bad times to be hungry for the good, thus becomes the first Australian captain since Bill Woodfull in 1934 to regain the Ashes in England. Put another way, David Gower, who by no stretch of the imagination has enjoyed an easy ride this summer, becomes the first English captain since Bob Wyatt to lose them on the same basis.

When the winning hit was made, Border, sat padded up on the team balcony, was swamped by team mates. If he couldn't have made the winning hit in person – and how many wished he had – then he was there in spirit. He, and his manager Bobby Simpson, have schemed and plotted this moment all summer. And before that. England have been outplayed, outwitted and outgunned by an Australian side blessed with skill, spirit, self-belief, good weather and good luck (although the more they planned the luckier they got).

Afterwards, Gower, appearing more relaxed in defeat than he has been all summer, immediately scotched reports that he might resign, and he still retains the backing of the England committee who appointed him for the entire series. But the stakes are different now. Gower has remained loyal to his ideals and his players, believing sincerely that they are the ones most capable of doing the job for him. That he has captained unimaginatively is only part of the story, for these players have not justified his faith. He has been let down badly, and the time is now here, with the pressure off him and with his hand forced by a variety of circumstances, for the rebuilding to begin.

And yet the game, a dead duck the previous evening, still, on an uninterrupted day, went into its last-half hour. For this England can thank Jack Russell, a man, remember, who for a long time was not able to take the wicket-keeping spot that ought to have been his by right, because it was felt he couldn't bat. No longer.

By the time Merv Hughes put an end to the England second innings, it was tea time, and Russell walked off with 128 runs to his name – his maiden century not only in Tests but in all cricket, an achievement matched, among Englishmen, only by Billy Griffith against West Indies in 1948. With John Emburey, who made 64 of the grittiest runs of his career, Russell batted right through the morning session and eventually they added 142 for the seventh wicket – just one short of the record for a seventh-wicket stand against Australia set by Woolley and Vine in 1912 – and took the England total to 201. They had salvaged the innings. From the depths of 59 for 6 they restored respectability, and showed what might have been.

Indeed, had their partnership lasted another hour, the match might have been saved. Instead, after lunch Border took the new ball immediately it became available, Emburey went back to Alderman, and saw it skid low through his defences to hit off-stump. It was the crucial breakthrough, leaving one end open, and above all, putting time once more on Australia's side. Neil Foster hung around defiantly for 40 minutes before he too became a victim of Alderman – his 27th of the series – and walked, head bowed and looking close to tears, from an English test arena for the last time.

Russell by now had reached 96 (already his best-ever score, exceeding the 94 he made against Sri Lanka last season), but was in danger of being left high and dry, tantalisingly close to his hundred. But Fraser propped and cocked, and after five and a half hours at the crease, Russell

Scoreboard from Old Trafford

England

First Innings: 260 (R A Smith 143; G F Lawson 6 for 72).

Second Innings

		6s	4s	Mins	Balls
G A Gooch c Alderman b Lawson	13	–	2	51	23
T S Curtis c Boon b Alderman	0	–	–	6	2
R T Robinson lbw b Lawson	12	–	1	31	28
R A Smith c Healy b Alderman	1	–	–	5	8
*D I Gower c Marsh b Lawson	15	–	1	67	40
I T Botham lbw b Alderman	4	–	–	24	23
†R C Russell not out	128	–	14	353	293
J E Emburey b Alderman	64	–	10	221	183
N A Foster b Alderman	6	–	–	39	28
A R C Fraser c Marsh b Hohns	3	–	–	39	32
N G B Cook c Healy b Hughes	5	–	1	10	11
Extras (lb 6, w 2, nb 5)	13				
Total (110.4 overs)	**264**				

FALL OF WICKETS: 1–10, 2–25, 3–27, 4–28, 5–38, 6–59, 7–201, 8–223, 9–255.
BOWLING: Lawson 31–8–81–3 (w 2, nb 2); Alderman 27–7–66–5 (nb 5); Hohns 26–15–37–1; Hughes 14.4–2–45–1; Border 8–2–12–0; Waugh 4–0–17–0.

Australia

First Innings: 447 (S R Waugh 92, M A Taylor 85, D M Jones 69, A R Border 80).

Second Innings

		6s	4s	Mins	Balls
G R Marsh c Robinson b Emburey	31	–	1	95	94
M A Taylor not out	37	–	4	112	83
D C Boon not out	10	–	2	15	23
Extras (nb 3)	3				
Total (1 wkt, 32.5 overs)	**81**				

*A R Border, D M Jones, S R Waugh, †I A Healy, T V Hohns, M G Hughes, G F Lawson and T M Alderman did not bat.

FALL OF WICKETS: 1–62.
BOWLING: Foster 5–2–5–0; Fraser 10–0–28–0 (nb 3); Emburey 13–3–30–1; Cook 4.5–0–18–0.

Man of the match: G F Lawson.

turned Alderman off his hips for the single that took him to three figures. Border, a man who above all appreciates honest endeavour, shook him warmly by the hand.

With Hohns and Hughes cleaning things up, it left Australia to score 78 to win in an hour and 20 minutes plus 20 overs: more than enough time. Marsh and Taylor once more provided the foundations and added 62 for the first wicket before Marsh, with the game in the bag, swept

ABOVE Australian celebrations in the dressing-room at Old Trafford

LEFT Border savours the moment

Emburey to Robinson at deep square-leg. Maybe Border should have come in, but it was indicative of how much of a team effort it has been that he stuck to routine. There was just time for Taylor to score his 500th run of the series before Boon, after teasing out the final moments, clinched things.

Postscript

It was sad that some of the limelight was taken away. Allan Border and his Ashes-winning team deserved centre-stage for a magnificent achievement: instead, South Africa, just as it had probably been planned, dominated the final day.

Sixteen Englishmen, 15 of them current or former Test players, with the kind of timing that has not been a notable feature of English batting this summer, churlishly chose Australia's day to announce that they would be undertaking a six-week tour of South Africa next winter under the captaincy of Mike Gatting, the start of which would coincide exactly with England's official tour of West Indies. Nine of these players, Gatting, Chris Broad, Phil DeFreitas, Tim Robinson, John Emburey, Kim Barnett, Graham Dilley, Paul Jarvis, and Neil Foster, had already taken part in the Ashes series; Robinson, Emburey and Foster played in this Fourth Test. None has had conspicuous success; most have been abject failures.

It prompts a number of thoughts. First, do the South Africans know exactly what they are actually getting for their reported £100,000 per head. Have restrictions not been lifted on the coverage of these Tests?

Then again, do all the players, young and old – all bar four will be thirty plus when the tour leaves, but Foster will be 26, Jarvis 24, DeFreitas and Matthew Maynard 23 – fully appreciate the consequences? When Graham Gooch led the first rebel tour in 1982, the price we and his team paid was a three-year ban from Test cricket. But now, in a move designed to prevent the fragmentation of world cricket, the International Cricket Conference has agreed unanimously that the penalty for another such tour should be a minimum five-year ban. To return for a second tour, as these players are contracted to do, would involve an extra two-year ban. Seven years in all, to be effective from the player's last visit to South Africa. In other words, they will not be eligible for a Test match until 1998. Most will be too old by then – even the youngest will be well into their thirties.

A third point, though, is will they be overly missed anyway, and the answer has to be no, for if Ted Dexter's words before the fourth Test – that changes and rebuilding would follow a defeat – are to be heeded, then these are exactly the sort of players who would be replaced.

Now that all the speculation has become fact, the amount of subterfuge that can be seen – recruitment has been going on since May – accounts for much of the apparent preoccupation of many players during the series. One cricketer, not one of the 16, has said that the dressing room has been a dull, nervous place, totally lacking in spark or spirit. It's not hard now to see why.

Nor is it a coincidence, by the same token, that two, possibly *the* two English performances of the summer came from two players, Robin Smith and Jack Russell, with 11 Tests between them and everything to play for. Maiden centuries for both, each made in difficult circumstances. Only Lamb's Headingley blitz and Gower's defiance at Lord's can match them.

At Old Trafford the Australians showed yet again what a team game cricket can be, with the batsmen single-mindedly chiselling out the runs, led once more by the immaculate Steve Waugh and the remarkably consistent Mark Taylor, but this time including Allan Border making sure that his tenuous grip on the Ashes didn't slip. It left the bowlers, feeding from this, to do their stuff. Once more it was the old firm of Lawson and Alderman who punched the holes in England. Lawson had a superb game, his best of the tour without a shadow of doubt, and having had a wicketless breather in the first innings, Alderman chipped in with yet another five in the second. Five times now these two have taken five wickets or more in an innings this summer. No Englishman has yet done so and that in itself gives an idea of the gulf.

England now must look to the future. Gower

is to remain as captain, at least for the foreseeable future, and he could form the nucleus of a batting side with some or all of Smith, Gooch, and Lamb. Probably a mixture of heads old and wise but untainted by recent Tests – the likes of Peter Roebuck or Paul Parker, say – and fresh young blood might be required in the cauldron that is the Caribbean. In the meantime, there is a heaven-sent opportunity to find out much about the cricketing youth of this land – players such as Nasser Hussein, Mark Ramprakash, Mike Atherton and the Bicknell brothers, Darren and Martin; and for a new pace attack to be assembled, based around Angus Fraser, who after two Tests, will almost be classed as a veteran. The Ashes might have gone, but for England there is still much, perhaps all, to play for.

Fifth Cornhill Test Match

England v Australia,
Trent Bridge 10–14 August 1989

Match preview

In the circumstances, it will probably come as a shock in Pretoria to find that the Test series is able to continue in the face of the disruption, but England have the chance to redeem some pride, if nothing else. 'Cricket,' said David Gower before nets, 'has always been a game where players can at the same time perform for their own good and benefit the team.' In other words, it is a selfish business in which you hope the sum total will exceed the individual parts. Manage that and you get an Australian Ashes-winning side.

For four Tests, each member of Allan Border's team has been set a specific task, which without exception, batter or bowler, he has pursued rigorously and single-mindedly. The individuals have performed to their potential, but collectively it has been greater than that: the side has performed way above itself. That, in a nutshell, has been the difference between the two sides this summer.

It will not be easy for England to change now. Australia are on a magnificent high and are not likely to relax their grip. England, by contrast, were rock bottom after the Old Trafford defeat and the subsequent South African defections.

Yet out of the mayhem some good may yet emerge this summer. Of the new-look England squad which trotted round the Trent Bridge perimeter during practice, five – Mike Atherton, Devon Malcolm, Martyn Moxon, Eddie Hemmings and Greg Thomas – are unfamiliar with the debacle, and the first two innocent of England shipwrecks of any kind.

'When the Ashes were at stake,' continued Gower, 'there could have been no bigger incentive. Now it boils down to individuals wanting to put in a performance on a purely selfish basis. The next step for us is to turn all this into a unit in which we all know what we are going to do.'

Not everyone has Gower's optimism that it will happen in this Test. The Tote, for example, has been offering 7 to 1 against an England win, and even at those generous odds they do not anticipate getting knocked over in the rush. Indeed, the only thing that is likely to get knocked over today is third slip, if Malcolm and Thomas operate in tandem with the new ball and the bio-rhythms are not quite right.

The chances are that England will decide to leave out a spinner – probably Nick Cook – and play all their pace bowlers, although Ron Allsopp, the groundsman, feels the pitch could turn. Joking aside, the pace attack could be an intriguing prospect, for while Malcolm and Thomas are not noted for their accuracy they are as quick a pair of bowlers as England have assembled for some while.

Add to that David Lawrence, who began his

comeback from injury at the weekend, and the return to the fold of DeFreitas, and there is, looking forward to the winter, some light in the tunnel. Together, Malcolm and Thomas are capable of putting the game beyond England in the first hour, but they equally could steam-roller a batting line-up.

Interest in the England batting will centre largely on the performance of Atherton, the 21-year-old Lancastrian, who makes the side on the strength of testimony as to his temperament and technique, rather than his figures this season which give him an average of 31 and no century. That surely is the way to select Test sides.

Fifth Test, 1st day

Australia 301–0

Let us, with English readers in mind, begin with the good news from the first day of the Fifth Test, or as Micky Stewart prefers to think of it with the series lost, the first day of the bye. Devon Malcolm, erstwhile terror of Viv and his men this winter, bowled with considerable pace on his test debut; he quite literally struck a couple of body blows, imperilled neither short leg nor third slip as had been anticipated, and generally looked the most likely England bowler to run through the Australian batting. And sometime during the afternoon, Geoff Marsh played back to the leg spin of the other English debutant, Mike Atherton, and misread his googly. Angus Fraser beat the bat a couple of times. That's about it.

The rest of the day was lost in such a welter of statistics that it might have been a Bill Frindall Benefit match. Allan Border won the toss, decided to bat first, and Geoff Marsh and Mark Taylor, as they have done all series, walked out together to face the revamped England attack. When the last ball of the day was bowled by Eddie Hemmings on the dot of six o'clock, they were still at it. Taylor blocked it studiously,

turned smartly on his heels and marched towards the pavilion, joined at the trot by Marsh. They shook hands and disappeared to a standing ovation. Small wonder; Marsh had made 125 and Taylor 141 (highest Test scores for both). In the process they had added a little matter of 301 for the first wicket, with the prospect of more to come.

Exactly one hundred runs previously, Marsh had on-driven Hemmings for a single to register the highest opening stand by Australians in England since Bobby Simpson and Bill Lawry rendered England comatose at Old Trafford in 1964. Forty-four runs later, after the board had been nervously stuck on the same score for four overs, Taylor swept the same bowler to the square-leg boundary, and it became Australia's highest-ever opening partnership against England, beating the 244 scored by, of course, Simpson and Lawry, this time at Adelaide 24 years ago. Should they manage a further 23, they will have demoted to second place the 323 that Jack Hobbs and Wilfred Rhodes compiled in Melbourne in 1911–12 and established the highest opening stand in the 269 matches played between these two sides over 112 years. No wonder the champagne corks popped.

But there's more. They had also, in the process, become the first players to bat through an entire day's play in a Test in this country, the ninth pair in all, and only the third ever to do so on the first day. The last, indeed the only other Australians to do this were, yes, you've guessed it, Simpson and Lawry, at Bridgetown, Barbados in 1964–65. Both those old stagers were at the ground to witness the record, Simpson the Australians' coach and Lawry a TV commentator.

If the gulf that has existed in quality between the two sides all summer needed any further emphasis, then Marsh and Taylor provided it magnificently. The pitch could scarcely have been better suited to them – no pace, bounce generally on the low side of average – except occasionally from glorious Devon, when an overhead smash would have been the requisite stroke – and although Taylor edged a couple close but short of slip fielders early on and top-edged Botham fiercely between first and second

Scoreboard from Trent Bridge

Australia won toss

Australia

First Innings

	6s	4s	Mins	Balls
G R Marsh not out........................... 125	–	15	361	320
M A Taylor not out........................... 141	–	13	361	309
Extras (b 5, lb 15, w 1, nb 14)..... 35				
Total (0 wkt, 102 overs) 301				

D C Boon, *A R Border, D M Jones, S R Waugh, †I A Healy, T V Hohns, M G Hughes, G F Lawson and T M Alderman to bat.
BOWLING: Fraser 24–9–54–0 (nb 12); Malcolm 18–2–65–0 (w 1, nb 3); Botham 20–3–68–0; Hemmings 20–5–47–0; Cook 15–6–26–0; Atherton 5–0–21–0 (nb 2).

England

T S Curtis, M D Moxon, M A Atherton, R A Smith, *D I Gower, I T Botham, †R C Russell, E E Hemmings, A R C Fraser, D E Malcolm and N G B Cook.

Umpires: D R Shepherd and N T Plews.

slip, and there were several hearty and well-meant shouts for lbw against Marsh, including a very close one from Malcolm, it is hard to believe how little trouble they were in.

David Gower probably did as well as he might with the attack he had, shuffling his cards more and his feet less than so far in the series. But the game can make fools of you. In leaving Greg Thomas out, England were a seamer light; if he'd played they'd have been a spinner short. You cannot win.

It was a salutary lesson for England, but to their credit all the bowlers stuck to their task well as Australia moved relentlessly, almost indifferently past their milestones. But the batsmen, sound in defence, were so fast onto anything loose, that the innings never stagnated.

Apart from a brief spell during the afternoon when Marsh overtook Taylor, it was the left-hander who was always ahead, and sure enough he was first, after 263 minutes, to his century, his second of the series. This has been a marvellous series for Taylor, who has made a major contribution in all the matches with four half-centuries in addition to his hundreds, and he has now scored 642 runs in the series, which is

phenomenal by any standards. Marsh though has not had the happiest of times this year, without even a half-century to his name. Moreover, it is three years and 22 Tests since he last made a hundred, and he only had three in all, although curiously, given his demeanour and style, he has made a number of hundreds in limited-over internationals. He put things right half an hour after Taylor, gratefully scampering a sharp single to square-leg. In a summer of Australian triumph, that must have been a weight off his mind.

Fifth Test, 2nd day

Australia 560–5

It must be hard if you are a Test captain to look at the scoreboard, see it reading 560 for 5, have one of your players, Mark Taylor, in the pavilion with a double-century to his name, and realise that you have not had an especially good day at the office. But that is how Allan Border must have felt last night as he walked off having made 46 not out.

By the end of the first hour, Geoff Marsh and Mark Taylor had taken their opening stand to 329, the best start any skipper has ever enjoyed in England–Australia Tests. It should have provided the springboard to a total somewhere in excess of 600 by close of play. Instead, England, just as they were wondering whether they would ever contrive to take a wicket, took not only one, to break the stand, but another four as well: five wickets for 259 in the day, in fact, with the first three to Nick Cook, and then one apiece for Angus Fraser, the pick of the bowlers by a street, and Devon Malcolm, his first wicket in Test cricket. As that happened to be the prime scalp of Steve Waugh, without scoring, Micky Stewart, with his optimism, may even feel that it clinched a rare England triumph.

A spirited effort it may have been by England, but that is the degree of straw-clutching to which we have slumped. The reality, of course, is still that once more, England are on the wrong end of a stuffing, as the Australian machine rolls relentlessly on. Border will not close his innings yet, but even as things stand, England need 361 to avoid following on, and there is little need to remind everyone that they have not even reached 300 in the first innings since the First Test.

For Australia to make over 500 was merely a continuation of an almost unmatched sequence of first innings: their last seven Tests have brought first-innings totals of 401, 515, 601, 528, 424, 447 and now 560. Only Pakistan, once, have matched that run, and you wouldn't bet against that going in the final Test at the Oval.

Taylor's effort was also the continuation of what has been a phenomenal series by the standards of even, well, Bradman. His partnership with Marsh had come to grief after just over seven hours when the Australian vice-captain tried to swing a rare flighted ball from Cook from outside off stump to the open on-side spaces and instead top-edged a catch to Botham at slip. As it had coincided with the removal of his restrictive close fielders, one hopes a point had been made.

What usually happens in those situations is that the other partner gets out. Not Taylor. With Boon now, who, remember, had been sat padded-up for the duration of the stand, he added a further 101 for the second wicket, during which Taylor finally square-cut Hemmings for the boundary that took him to 200. When he was finally out for 219, stumped for the third time in four Test knocks (a weakness there!), he might have been thinking of 300 and beyond that, Sobers. Certainly there was time. Instead he can be content with 720 runs in the series. Of Australians, only Bradman (three times) has made more against England.

Boon played the most adventurous innings of the day, scoring a brisk 73, but survived two chances in the process, the second of which dislocated the fourth finger on Ian Botham's right hand, as he dived for a screamer off Malcolm at second slip. But he too advanced down the pitch to Cook and will have been as surprised as anyone to see the ball turn and bounce. Russell once more completed the honours.

Scoreboard from Trent Bridge

Australia

First Innings

		6s	4s	Mins	Balls
G R Marsh c Botham b Cook	138	–	15	426	382
M A Taylor st Russell b Cook	219	–	23	554	461
D C Boon st Russell b Cook	73	–	9	210	183
*A R Border not out	46	–	6	165	111
D M Jones c Gower b Fraser	22	–	3	51	44
S R Waugh c Gower b Malcolm	0	–	–	13	8
†I A Healy not out	5	–	–	8	3
Extras (b 6, lb 23, w 3, nb 25)	57				
Total (5 wkts, 194 overs)	**560**				

T V Hohns, M G Hughes, G F Lawson and T M Alderman to bat.

FALL OF WICKETS: 1–329, 2–430, 3–502, 4–543, 5–553.

BOWLING: Fraser 46–17–91–1 (nb 14); Malcolm 38–2–141–1 (w 2, nb 12); Botham 30–4–103–0 (w 1); Hemmings 33–9–81–0; Cook 40–10–91–3; Atherton 7–0–24–0 (nb 2).

England

T S Curtis, M D Moxon, M A Atherton, R A Smith, *D I Gower, I T Botham, †R C Russell, E E Hemmings, A R C Fraser, D E Malcolm and N G B Cook.

In the evening, Border, Jones and Waugh all struggled to break free, and the new ball brought further breakthroughs, as Jones ballooned a catch apparently from bat and pad to point, and Waugh, helmeted for the first time in the series, a tribute possibly to Malcolm's pace but more likely to his unpredictability, flicked that bowler off his toes to square leg. Gower took both catches.

Yet it remains a curious effort by Australia. At the end of the first day of the series at Headingley, they had made 207 for 3; by the end of the second they had taken that to 580 for 6. Here, with the pressure off, the series won and nothing at stake, the way was clear for similar expansion. Instead, only 64 runs came in the morning, 95 in the afternoon and exactly 100 in the evening session.

Some credit must be given to the England bowlers, who persisted without flagging. For Cook to bowl 40 overs in the manner he does and concede fewer than 100 runs is remarkable – he must bowl an awful lot of dot-balls to compensate for the one bad delivery per over. Hemmings too was tidy, which is not a quality that has always been in evidence this summer. But the effort of Fraser, who worked his way through 46 overs at under two runs per over, was stupendous: the very essence of Test cricket. At last England have a bowler who has the control, accuracy and heart to make batting, if not necessarily hazardous on a good pitch, then at least a test of patience.

Fifth Test, 3rd day

Australia 602–6 dec
England 246–9

Remember the story of the boxer, suffering a fearful battering, who has once more struggled, bloodied, back to his corner. 'Don't worry,' his second says cheerfully, 'you can do it. He hasn't touched you yet.' 'Well,' the boxer says with a sigh as the bell sounds for the next round, 'keep an eye on the ref because someone's belting the hell out of me.'

Every time England have walked onto the field for this summer's six-rounder they have done so with a jaunty step, heads up, and jingoism ringing in their ears. Yet at the end of each day they have trudged off with another cauliflower ear. Someone, they must finally have realised, no matter what they are told, is belting the hell out of them as well, and he wears a baggy green cap.

Each Test match, it seems, a new low is reached. Headingley, the first match of the series, which at the time was regarded as a national disaster, is increasingly looking like a minor triumph by comparison with what has followed. On Saturday, at Trent Bridge, just after lunch, the season reached rock bottom. For two days and the best part of an hour, England had foot-slogged their way as Australia relentlessly accumulated their highest total of the series; Allan Border, who has been a magnificent general – as good now, perhaps, as any that have toured here – has scarcely missed a trick,

however subtle, and he made a point of easing past the 601 of Headingley beore calling a halt at 602 for 6, with himself, already second only to Sunil Gavaskar among Test run-makers, 65 not out. He might have gone on – in what must have been a new definition of optimism, a spectator was heard to suggest that Border would not fancy batting last on a turning pitch – but the moment was well chosen.

In the course of the innings, it has taken England seven hours and seven minutes of sweat before they even broke the opening stand of Geoff Marsh and Mark Taylor, and it was half an hour short of two days before they had taken four wickets. It took Terry Alderman just one over to put that in perspective as Martyn Moxon edged his fourth ball low to second slip, where Steve Waugh picked up his first catch not only of the series but of the tour; and then two balls later, Mike Atherton, in his first Test innings, plunged forward down the line of off stump, the ball came up middle, and that was that.

What was Atherton doing coming in at three? The captain and manager had asked him how he felt about it and he said he would be happy to bat in the position in which he felt comfortable. But of course he would have said that; he is new, would want to impress, and to do otherwise would have implied lack of confidence on his part. The management were also, for similar reasons, in a difficult situation, because to have shifted him down the order might have been interpreted by the player as a lack of confidence in him. So common sense should have prevailed. Better for Gower to have taken the number three position himself and let Atherton acclimatise at five.

After an hour, it had become irrelevant in any case because two more batsmen, Tim Curtis, who got a brute of a ball which skidded through low, and Gower himself, playing a wild slash outside off stump, were also gone. The scoreboard read 37 for 4. Never has Gower looked greyer or more dejected than when he walked off to an embarrassed, muted, foot-shuffling pavilion.

So thank goodness then for Robin Smith, the polite, quiet-spoken young man who is rapidly becoming an assassin with the bat. At the crease, after one over, he launched a counter-assault on the Australian bowling of a ferocity and power matched only perhaps by Allan Lamb's century at Leeds. It was not an innings born out of desperation, but conceived by a player with boundless natural ability, a technique on which he has worked long hours to rectify a tendency to fall over to the off side and hit across his pad, a will of iron and tungsten nerves.

But above all, the game is fresh to him. This is only his seventh Test match, and life is a challenge. Had Gatting and Lamb not been injured at various times, he might not even have played, such has been the myopic selection policy. The successes of the series have been him, Russell and Fraser, all new to the game, and that is not a coincidence.

From the moment Smith announced himself by twice rifling Alderman back past the bowler, to the bloodthirsty pull-shot three hours later through mid-wicket off Hohns's leg-spin that brought him his 16th boundary and with it his second Test hundred in consecutive matches, he was in total command. He had struck the bad ball as hard as any England player can have done for years, bottom hand like a pile-driver, slamming Merv Hughes in the process for five boundaries in 10 balls – no question who is on top in this clash of personalities – and rendering David Boon doolally at short leg when a pull struck and fractured his fielding helmet. What it might have done to Boon's head had the helmet not been there does not bear thinking about.

Yet as with the Australian innings this summer, he could not have flourished without support. With Botham unable to bat until late because of the effect of his finger dislocation, and then severely handicapped when he did, Russell stayed for 23 overs, Hemmings for 26 more, and then later when Smith, by self-confession having retreated into his shell when he should have carried on as he was, played what he called a 'nothing shot' to the looser for the new spell by Alderman, and was caught at the wicket, Fraser used up 21 more. It was never enough – England, at 246 for 9, still need 157 runs to avoid following on – but it was crumbs on a gloomy day.

If further comfort is needed, however, it may

Scoreboard from Trent Bridge

Australia

First Innings

		6s	4s	Mins	Balls
G R Marsh c Botham b Cook	138	–	15	426	382
M A Taylor st Russell b Cook	219	–	23	554	461
D C Boon st Russell b Cook	73	–	9	210	183
*A R Border not out	65	–	7	221	143
D M Jones c Gower b Fraser	22	–	3	51	44
S R Waugh c Gower b Malcolm	0	–	–	13	8
†I A Healy b Fraser	5	–	–	12	7
T V Hohns not out	19	–	2	52	45
Extras (b 6, lb 23, w 3, nb 29)	61				
Total (6 wkts dec, 206.3 overs)	**602**				

M G Hughes, G F Lawson and T M Alderman did not bat.

FALL OF WICKETS: 1–329, 2–430, 3–502, 4–543, 5–553, 6–560.

BOWLING: Fraser 52.3–18–108–2 (nb 15); Malcolm 44–2–166–1 (w 2, nb 17); Botham 30–4–103–0 (w 1); Hemmings 33–9–81–0; Cook 40–10–91–3; Atherton 7–0–24–0 (nb 2).

England

First Innings

		6s	4s	Mins	Balls
T S Curtis lbw b Alderman	2	–	–	25	16
M D Moxon c Waugh b Alderman	0	–	–	2	3
M A Atherton lbw b Alderman	0	–	–	1	2
R A Smith c Healy b Alderman	101	–	16	205	150
*D I Gower c Healy b Lawson	11	–	–	31	25
†R C Russell c Healy b Lawson	20	–	1	91	63
E E Hemmings b Alderman	38	–	5	101	83
A R C Fraser b Hohns	29	–	3	85	55
I T Botham c Waugh b Hohns	12	–	1	54	49
N G B Cook not out	1	–	–	16	14
D E Malcolm not out	1	–	–	5	5
Extras (lb 18, nb 13)	31				
Total (9 wkts, 75 overs)	**246**				

FALL OF WICKETS: 1–1, 2–1, 3–14, 4–37, 5–119, 6–172, 7–214, 8–243, 9–244.

BOWLING: Alderman 19–2–69–5 (nb 11); Lawson 21–5–57–2 (nb 1); Hohns 17–8–39–2; Hughes 7–0–40–0 (nb 2); Waugh 11–4–23–0 (nb 1).

be found in the fact that had the game been in Australia next year, things would have been decidedly worse. In an attempt to curb no-balls, it has been decided there that not only shall transgressions be worth two runs henceforth (a compromise on the four that was suggested), but that they shall be added to any runs scored. In the Australian innings, England bowled 34 no-balls, of which five conceded runs. Under the

Smith comes off best this time in his on-going personal battle with Merv Hughes

LEFT Steve Waugh picks up Martyn Moxon off the bowling of Alderman in the first innings at Trent Bridge

RIGHT Moxon receives an instant reaction to his dismissal from a disillusioned spectator

new rule, 39 extra runs would have accrued to the Australian total. We must be thankful for small mercies.

Fifth Test, 4th day

Australia 602–6 dec
England 255 and 117
Australia won by an innings and 180 runs

It was just another day in the Australian office. The fifth Test match went the way of numbers one, two and four shortly after tea on the fourth day, when Merv Hughes slid a near full-toss through the groping defence of Devon Malcolm and hit the base of the stumps to reduce England in their second innings to 167 for 9. For a moment there was hesitation on the field with players unsure whether to pull a celebratory stump from the ground; Ian Botham, despite his dislocated finger had propped up the innings for almost an hour in the England first innings, and had sat padded up, ready to bat in the second if the weather looked like intervening. He failed to appear, and the game was Australia's by an innings and 180 runs, the greatest margin they have ever beaten England by in this country. One hour later, the ground was flooded by a thunder shower.

Humiliation. It was England's lowest score of the summer. As the day wore on, there was similar speculation to that following the defeat in the Fourth Test at Old Trafford: that had it not been for the announcement of the South African tour, Gower may have made an emotive and hasty decision that enough was enough. Gower has denied that he had any such notion though, and after the match he reiterated his decision to see things through, although the inference is that his position might be considered by all concerned after the final Test at the Oval. He confesses to being depressed, as well he might be, but continues to stress that he is trying to

isolate what is happening from what he believes is possible. That is no easy thing.

Once more there was a bowling lesson for all aspiring England bowlers, this time not from Terry Alderman but from Geoff Lawson. Until the fourth Test, the New South Wales captain had struggled for rhythm and pace. But he took confidence-boosting wickets in the defeat of Gloucestershire before Manchester, and since then has got better and better until yesterday he ran in as if on nylon bearings. That his figures – 2 for 51 – were the worst of the four bowlers used by Allan Border in no way diminishes his performance. It was outstanding fast-bowling.

But there can be no excuse for a Test side to get bowled out on an easy-paced pitch (although the bounce was becoming low) in under 56 overs. The resilience, with a couple of exceptions, was paper-thin once the first two wickets had fallen for 13. Mike Atherton, who had failed to score in the first innings demonstrated his aptitude for occupying the crease by batting for almost three hours for his 47 runs, Martyn Moxon took 69 minutes over 18, and Robin Smith an hour for 26. That apart, the only contribution of any substance came during a late thrash from Eddie Hemmings. When the glimpse of the future consists of watching a 40-year old off-spinner gathering 73 runs over the two innings, the second highest English aggregate in the game, it speaks volumes.

It was not, to be fair, the best of starts. It had taken Australia 11 balls, at the expense of 9 runs, including a six over long-on from Devon Malcolm, to finish off the England first innings. At 255 all out, they still required a daunting 347 to avoid an innings defeat.

They tried to be positive about things. With Botham out of action, the rationale was to shore up the middle order with solidity, in the form of Moxon, and sock 'em with a right–left combination just as Australia had been doing to them. Gower's flit up the order (for he, not Jack-Russell, was the left-hander about whom we are speaking) was not a success. He punched his first ball from Alderman through mid-off for four, and stole a single off the second to get to the other end. To the third ball of Lawson's opening over, he shouldered arms, the ball came back at him a fraction and clipped the top of the off stump. It was, hit or miss, too close to leave, but it did sum up his series. Three overs later, Curtis became Alderman's 16th lbw victim out of 33 wickets thus far.

But just as Smith, Fraser and Russell have given some hope for the future, so did the performance of Atherton. He stands up tall at the crease, bat raised but not excessively, and plays straight. He was off his pair with his first ball, and in a stay of 39 overs, hit three boundaries, the best of which was a back-foot forcing shot off Alderman with the elbow-high flourish of Boycott. During his stay, he had seen Smith yorked by Hughes, Moxon bowled by a shooter from Alderman, and Russell bowled off-stump by Lawson playing a horrendous leg-side shovel that belied his batting in the series. One over later, Atherton had gone, hitting a low return catch to Hohns.

Now generally speaking, this has been an even-tempered series, so it was unfortunate to see things boil over when Hemmings on 9, edged Lawson to Waugh at third slip who, picking the ball up close to the half-volley, claimed the catch. Hemmings, as is his right if unsure that the catch has been taken cleanly, stayed his ground, and the umpires decided that they too were uncertain it had been taken legitimately. So Hemmings stayed, and the air turned blue, with the atmosphere not cooling down until Border slammed his own men during tea. They can have had no gripe though, for Mark Taylor did exactly the same at Lord's, although he was subsequently given out.

Hemmings took advantage of his let-off with some yeoman blows, mostly at the expense of Lawson, hitting five fours, although losing Fraser on the way, deceived by Hohns's top-spinner, but after tea, he played back to Hughes and was on his way before the finger was up. To Hughes fell the coup de grace.

Once more then, the selectors have to look forward. The Oval, as Dexter says, is in principle an opportunity to do something about it, but then so was this Test. In practice, they may be forced, purely to be consistent with stated policies, to stick as closely as they can to this side.

One man who is sure to be missing is Botham,

Scoreboard from Trent Bridge

Australia

First innings: 602 for 6 dec (G R Marsh 138, M A Taylor 219, D C Boon 73, A R Border 65 not out).

England

First Innings

	6s	4s	Mins	Balls
T S Curtis lbw b Alderman	2	–	–	25	16
M D Moxon c Waugh b Alderman	0	–	–	2	3
M A Atherton lbw b Alderman	0	–	–	1	2
R A Smith c Healy b Alderman	101	–	16	205	150
*D I Gower c Healy b Lawson	11	–	–	31	25
†R C Russell c Healy b Lawson	20	–	1	91	63
E E Hemmings b Alderman	38	–	5	101	83
A R C Fraser b Hohns	29	–	3	85	55
I T Botham c Waugh b Hohns	12	–	1	54	49
N G B Cook not out	2	–	–	22	15
D E Malcolm c Healy b Hughes	9	1	–	11	15
Extras (lb 18, nb 13)	31				
Total (76.5 overs)	**255**				

FALL OF WICKETS: 1–1, 2–1, 3–14, 4–37, 5–119, 6–172, 7–214, 8–243, 9–244.
BOWLING: Alderman 19–2–69–5 (nb 11); Lawson 21–5–57–2 (nb 1); Hohns 18–8–48–2; Hughes 7.5–0–40–1 (nb 2); Waugh 11–4–23–0 (nb 1).

Second Innings

	6s	4s	Mins	Balls
*D I Gower b Lawson	5	–	1	6	5
T S Curtis lbw b Alderman	6	–	1	20	10
M A Atherton c and b Hohns	47	–	3	172	127
R A Smith b Hughes	26	–	4	62	44
M D Moxon b Alderman	18	–	3	69	48
†R C Russell b Lawson	1	–	–	16	14
E E Hemmings lbw Hughes	35	–	5	58	48
A R C Fraser b Hohns	1	–	–	15	9
N G B Cook not out	7	–	–	41	27
D E Malcolm b Hughes	5	–	1	5	9
I T Botham absent injured					
Extras (b 3, lb 6, w 1, nb 6)	16				
Total (55.3 overs)	**167**				

FALL OF WICKETS: 1–5, 2–13, 3–67, 4–106, 5–114, 6–120, 7–134, 8–160, 9–167.
BOWLING: Alderman 16–6–32–2 (nb 5); Lawson 15–3–51–2 (nb 1); Hughes 12.3–1–46–3 (nb 2); Hohns 12–3–29–2 (w 1).

Man of the Match: M A Taylor (Australia)

who has severe ligament damage to his hand. He has, however, told Dexter that in the absence of experience available to the selectors, he is ready and willing to tour West Indies, an about-turn

RIGHT Lawson and Hemmings exchange pleasantries after Steve Waugh had claimed a slip catch. Hemmings did not walk, the umpire said not out, and Lawson's exact words were splashed across the back pages the following morning

LEFT '... And this is where you sit if you're out for 0.' Captain Gower with new boys Mike Atherton and Martyn Moxon

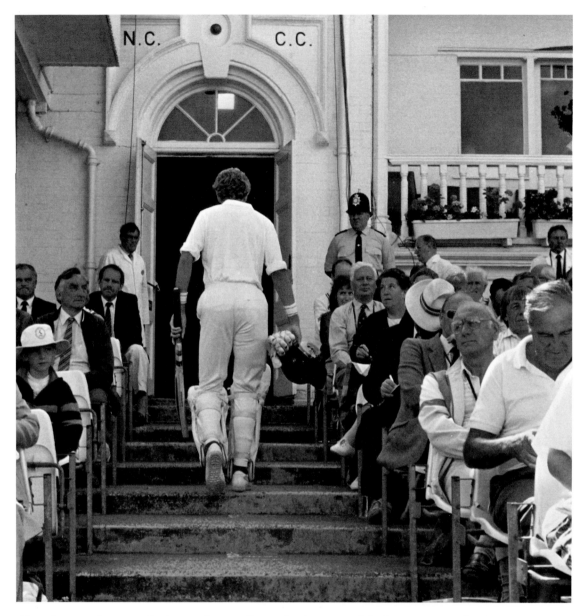

Glum faces in the Trent Bridge pavilion as Gower, having opened the batting, is out for 5.

of his previous notion not to tour again. 'Is that good news?' Gower was asked. 'If anybody is available it's good news,' was Gower's reply. Let's hope so.

Postscript

Down, down, ever down. How much further does this particular aircraft have to plunge before the pilot hauls back on the controls, lifts the nose and begins the long haul back to cruising altitude?

The Fifth Test was a match for the statistician, so we might as well toss in a few more. The win over Sri Lanka last season would not normally rate a mention in the same breath as an Ashes series but it is so rapidly acquiring the status of an historic day that August 30th, 1988 will probably be celebrated every year along with Trafalgar, a similarly one-eyed victory. It remains the only plus in a sequence of 24 matches since the win in Melbourne almost three years ago. At risk of repetition, England have now won just three of their last 39 Test matches, and have lost 19.

Nor is David Gower's captaincy record anything to be proud of; he has now lost 10 of his last 11 matches in charge. No other captain in Test history can match that.

So what lessons can be learned from yet another debacle? The first, and surely the most important, is that the future lies with youth, not in attempting to flog a last bit of life from a tired body of cricketers. It is typical that Ian Botham has decided that his country needs him and has made himself available for the West Indies tour. Equally, with a record against West Indies that fails to match his deeds against all the other countries, he probably feels he has a point to prove. To be called 'great', you have to have done it against the best, and discrepancies such as Botham's record contains, can create doubt about the merit of even a player of his standing.

The fact that he is available though – and there is even talk, for goodness sake, of him being made captain – does not mean he has to be selected, and the future lies elsewhere. Robin Smith has already more than amply demonstrated what youthful ambition, allied to skill, can do. He has had to fight to gain acceptance into the cabal; now, suddenly he is the main England batsman. Similarly Jack Russell and Angus Fraser have forced their way through the ranks. Their success comes not only from their abilities but from their hunger to succeed. Their enthusiasm for Test cricket, even in a losing side, has as yet become untainted by either complacency or the dispirited hammerings that England have endured. Many of Border's team underwent such an experience and look at them now.

To those three can now probably be added Mike Atherton. The list of players who made 0 on their Test debut and went on to better, even great things, is long – in 1954, Ken Barrington got a duck against the South Africans on this same Trent Bridge ground, and Len Hutton did so at Lord's years earlier against New Zealand.

What Atherton demonstrated in his innings of 47 was an aptitude to occupy the crease and accumulate; the temperament, having failed in the first innings, not to have openly appeared nervous even if he was; and the technique to cope with quality bowling. It showed more of his character than would have been evident had his scores been reversed.

Will the selectors have learned the lesson by the time the last Test side is chosen? Out in the shires, Nasser Hussain goes from strength to strength, and Botham's injury provides an opportunity for further experiment, although knowing him, he'll make a miracle recovery and make life awkward again.

As we probably know all we need to know about Tim Curtis, England could go into the last Test with a side which, however raw, has been selected with positive motives, and no one will have cause to gripe if they fail to beat a superbly-drilled side. If they stick to their guns though, and continue offering opportunities to players who clearly aren't up to the mark – and history suggests they might – then God help their credibility.

Sixth Cornhill Test Match

England v Australia
The Oval, 24–29 August 1989

Match Preview

England's fortunes have been reflected in some odd places this year, but when you see that a ditty called 'I Just Don't Have The Heart' has crept into the Top Ten singles chart to join 'Losing My Mind' and 'You're History' you know that the malaise has reached most levels.

It scarcely bears repeating that England this summer have been taken for mugs in all departments, beginning with selection, progressing through organisation and captaincy, and finishing with the churlishly unbalanced manner in which Lady Luck has bestowed her favours. England's plans, well and ill-conceived alike, have consistently been disrupted by a myriad of injuries, while Australia have been able to field a side unchanged since the Second Test at Lord's. Heartbreaking is not the word for it.

And the pop charts provide a neat encapsulation of it all. 'Poison' roars Alice Cooper, a mite o.t.t., but on the right lines. 'Batman' may be flavour of the month, but only Robin has produced runs regularly, with jokers too often made of the rest.

Of the bowlers who have actually made it onto the field, Angus Fraser alone has matched the Australians for consistency. 'Swing The Mood' and 'Cuts Both Ways', on the other hand, sound like fair reflections of Geoff Lawson and Terry Alderman, the latter, with 34 wickets this series,

needing only 8 more to equal his own record for an Ashes series.

Jason Donovan, an Australian Greg Campbell look-alike, can readily supply 'Ten Good Reasons' for this although Micky Stewart has come up with almost as many, ranging from the quality of pitches and the dominance of overseas players to the general structure of cricket in this country. 'Blame It On The Boogie' is not one he has used yet, but give him time.

As the Blow Monkeys point out, 'Choices' have not helped the cause. Selection policy this summer, until it was too late, has generally lacked imagination and obvious thought, and 'Wouldn't Change a Thing' – at least not unless forced to by injury – might have been written as a signature tune for Ted Dexter and Co.

Changes have had to be made of course, right up to the eve of this final Test. Derek Pringle and Alan Igglesden, something old and something new, became the latest bowlers to be drafted into the side, after the injuries to Fraser and DeFreitas.

Pringle, dear old Pring, is a veteran of 20 Tests and probably almost as many omissions afterwards, and has been everyone's favourite scapegoat. But he is currently enjoying his best season yet with the ball and has taken more wickets (86) than anyone in the land.

Igglesden by contrast is a 24-year-old 6′6″ beanpole from Kent, who has just about got a thousand overs behind him in his first-class career, although if he plays, as he surely must, he might, judging by the bleached belter and brown outfield which are awaiting, have added substantially to that come Tuesday. 'He moved it away from the bat earlier in the season', said Stewart, and to survive intact here he might need to do it again.

The unlucky – or should it be lucky – men to be left out on the day (it really does look unforgiving out in the middle, and will be a great toss to win) will be a bowler, probably Hemmings, and one of the two new Essex batsmen – Stephenson, if Gower can be persuaded to open; Hussain if not, which either way is a pity.

For England's revamped side the game promises to be what is euphemistically called a 'character-builder'. But they will at least play with pride and enthusiasm, a pair of commodities that have not been too evident this year. Meanwhile, one last comment from the charts. Some years ago, the aforementioned Mr Cooper produced an anarchic anthem entitled 'Schools Out'. Such has been the Aussie swagger that had he released it this season, it would presumably have carried 'lbw Alderman' in brackets as well. It's been that sort of year.

Sixth test, 1st day

Australia 325–3

The life expectancy of a soldier in the trenches must have been similar to that of the career prospects of an England Test cricketer this summer. And to be honest, this series has finally taken on the aspect of that form of warfare, with man after man of Blighty's best being propelled by the bunkered generals enthusiastically in against the rampant Aussies, only for them to be ruthlessly machine-gunned down and replaced by the next bunch of hapless youngsters going over the top. 'Goodbye, Picca Dilley . . .' as they probably sang on the way to the Oval yesterday.

It promised to be a tough day for someone. Even before play the weather was burning up another furnace, the pitch, stark against a verdant square, was as smooth and pale as alabaster; the Oval outfield brown as toast and hard as concrete underfoot. An ideal day in fact for any captain to win the toss, sit back and enjoy his batsmen filling their boots.

But it was Alan Border, not David Gower, who was the lucky man, and by the end of the day, a familiar pattern had emerged, with Australia poised today yet again to put the game totally out of England's reach. Their 325 for 3 represents, in terms of runs, the most productive first day of the summer – more so even than at Trent Bridge, when Geoff Marsh and Mark Taylor had made 301 of their record opening stand. It also means that they are well on target to become the first Test side ever to top 400 in eight consecutive first innings. There were good runs for all the batsmen this time except Marsh, a centurion last time out; Taylor, with the inevitability that must have surrounded Bradman, took his series aggregate to 791 with 71, his seventh score over fifty, which includes a century and a double century; David Boon, bristling like Merv's moustache, made 46 before becoming a victim of his own exuberance; and Border has battled his way to an unbeaten 66 – no betting against him getting his first hundred of the series on the second day.

But all these pale into insignificance alongside a glorious century from Dean Jones, who quite simply tore the England bowling to shreds. By the close, he had made 114 not out from a paltry 141 balls, and his century – the sixth of his career – was, at 119 balls, the fastest of the summer. There have been some special innings this summer – Waugh, Taylor, Gower, Lamb, Smith, and indeed Jones himself but this one ranks high among them. In partnership with Border, Jones has added 176 for the fourth wicket in only 40 overs, which Einsteins will note is a rate close to $4\frac{1}{2}$ runs per over. At this rate, Australia could have 600 by teatime on Friday, and then who knows what.

It would be wrong to suggest, though, that

Scoreboard from The Oval

Australia won toss

Australia

First Innings

	6s	4s	Mins	Balls
G R Marsh c Igglesden b Small	17	–	2	79	62
M A Taylor c Russell b Igglesden ...	71	–	4	163	125
D C Boon c Atherton b Small	46	–	6	124	90
*A R Border not out	66	–	10	204	129
D M Jones not out	114	–	16	162	141
Extras (b 1, lb 4, nb 6)	11				
Total (3 wkts, 90 overs)	**325**				

S R Waugh, †I A Healy, T V Hohns, M G Hughes, G F Lawson and T M Alderman to bat.

FALL OF WICKETS: 1–48, 2–130, 3–149.

BOWLING: Small 23–3–89–2; Igglesden 15–0–58–1 (nb 6); Pringle 14–4–44–0 (nb 1); Capel 10–2–39–0; Cook 25–5–78–0; Atherton 1–0–10–0; Gooch 2–1–2–0.

England

G A Gooch, J P Stephenson, M A Atherton, R A Smith, *D I Gower, D J Capel, †R C Russell, D R Pringle, G C Small, A P Igglesden and N G B Cook.

Umpires: H D Bird and K E Palmer.

England were abject. In fact, until midway through the afternoon, the England attack – Hemmings and Hussain were the men left out – had acquitted itself well, with Australia at 149 for 3 and two new batsmen in.

Marsh and Taylor had added 48 cautious runs in 20 overs for the first wicket, useful of course but small beer compared to Nottingham, before Marsh pulled ineffectively at a short, but scarcely dangerous ball from Gladstone Small, and spliced a gentle catch to Alan Igglesden at mid-wicket.

Small was able to extract some bounce from the pitch, as Boon found out when his first ball, a bit quicker this time, hit him on the right shoulder. But it merely served to wake him up, and he and Taylor added 81 in 20 overs, with Boon punching his boundaries square of the wicket.

Taylor was next to go, slashing at the sort of wide ball, from Igglesden, that he has been leaving all series, and edging to Russell; over-confident maybe, on the perfect surface, with the end of the tour in sight. 19 runs later and it was Boon back in the pavilion, and in a summer

where little credit has gone to Gower for his captaincy, a modicum now. Two overs previously, he had moved Atherton from square-leg to third slip. Now Boon drove at Small and the edge flew fast straight to Atherton.

It was the start of the best English cricket of the day, with Small aggressive while accurate, and Cook regaining some of his confidence and forcing Border, in particular, to work overtime. Border, though, had the presence of mind to recognise that Jones was in prime form and fed him the strike. Jones responded with a blaze of strokes and hard running. He reached his fifty from 54 balls with his eighth four, on-driven off Pringle, and his hundred an hour and a quarter later with his thirteenth and fourteenth off consecutive balls from Igglesden.

Already then, a win seems out of England's reach. To salvage anything, they must make substantial inroads with the new ball tomorrow, but one fears the worst.

Sixth Test, 2nd day

Australia 468
England 1–1

There have not been many days – no, sessions – this series in which England can genuinely claim to have bettered Australia. Even Micky Stewart, whose optimism in the past has stretched to claiming a victory, in terms of days won, from a series actually lost to Pakistan, has only put an England label on one day and a tenuous half.

But until a final, awful, Machiavellian twist applied a dampener, matched by the subsequent drizzle which ended play for the day shortly after three o'clock, English supporters – there are still some, judging by the packed Oval – who, having been promised a binge on success have instead suffered starvation rations this summer, would have been forgiven if they had broken out into a chorus of 'Rule Britannia'.

For not only did Australia, 325 for three overnight, fail to get the prescribed, almost obligatory 600 plus, they didn't even make 500. In fact – and this is not a spoof – they were bowled out for a paltry 468, an addition of 143. To do so, after Dean Jones and Alan Border had taken their fourth wicket partnership from 176 to 196 in the first three-quarters of an hour, the England bowlers took the last seven Aussie wickets for 123, inspired by an impeccable performance from Gladstone Small that lent a lie to his figures, and a neat bit of mopping up by Derek Pringle, who nipped in for four of them.

Four of the wickets, those of Border (76), Jones (122), Steve Waugh (14) and Ian Healy (44) went down for 90 in a heady morning session bettered only once this summer, when the final session of the third day at Old Trafford yielded five Australian wickets for 90.

It would be an over-simplification, though, to place credit for the day's events purely at the door of more competitive bowling, important as it may have been. Small and Pringle in particular, but also Igglesden and Capel, were undoubtedly helped by the prevailing conditions. On the first day, they had been perfect for batting: bright light, a belting pitch with pace and even bounce, and wide open spaces into which to dispatch the ball. However, take the same pitch but add a moody, brooding cloud cover, and the balance of power shifts. Suddenly, with bowlers mentally uplifted by the change in the weather, the pace and bounce in the pitch, allied to a modicum of movement, instead become a threat to the batsmen. The England bowlers for the most part made full use of the chance given them.

It was a different Border and Jones from the free-scoring pair of the first day, when they ran England ragged. With the second new ball taken immediately, Small sent down maiden after probing maiden, and Igglesden was steady. The first wicket, that of Border, can be directly attributed to this attrition because the visibly agitated Australian captain, having hit just one thunderous cover-drive off Igglesden in adding 10 runs to his overnight 66, then tried to pull David Capel's first ball, and gloved a simple looping catch to the keeper. Border, who in spite of his

Scoreboard from The Oval

Australia

First Innings

		6s	4s	Mins	Balls
G R Marsh c Igglesden b Small	17	–	2	79	62
M A Taylor c Russell b Igglesden	71	–	4	163	125
D C Boon c Atherton b Small	46	–	6	124	90
*A R Border c Russell b Capel	76	–	11	245	156
D M Jones c Gower b Small	122	–	17	213	180
S R Waugh b Igglesden	14	–	1	44	28
†I A Healy c Russell b Pringle	44	–	6	57	44
T V Hohns c Russell b Pringle	30	–	4	97	62
M G Hughes lbw Pringle	21	–	3	45	42
G F Lawson b Pringle	2	–	–	9	8
T M Alderman not out	6	–	1	16	10
Extra (b 1, lb 9, nb 9)	19				
Total (132.3 overs)	**468**				

FALL OF WICKETS: 1-48, 2-130, 3-149, 4-345, 5-347, 6-386, 7-409, 8-447, 9-453.
BOWLING: Small 40–8–141–3; Igglesden 24–2–91–2 (nb 11); Pringle 24.3–6–70–4 (nb 1); Capel 16–2–66–1; Cook 25–5–78–0; Atherton 1–0–10–0; Gooch 2–1–2–0.

England

First Innings

		6s	4s	Mins	Balls
G A Gooch lbw b Alderman	0	–	–	3	3
J P Stephenson not out	0	–	–	10	4
M A Atherton not out	0	–	–	6	4
Extras (nb 1)	1				
Total (1 wkt, 1.4 overs)	**1**				

R A Smith, *D I Gower, D J Capel, †R C Russell, D R Pringle, G C Small, A P Igglesden and N G B Cook to bat.

FALL OF WICKET: 1–1.
BOWLING: Alderman 1–0–1–1 (nb 1); Lawson 0.4–0–0–0.

unobtrusive consistency, has not scored a Test century for 12 Tests now, was not best pleased.

Nor was Jones who followed him one over later, although he was the victim of a superb piece of cricket. He had added only another eight runs to his score, struggling, like Border, with his timing, when Small bowled him a delivery that pitched on the stumps, bounced and left him. The catch went fast and low to Gower's left at first slip, and the England captain, seeing it late, took it one-handed almost after it was past him at grass height.

And joy was unconfined when, by lunch, Waugh, after reminding Capel sternly of his prowess against the short, wide ball, had played a straight, bouncing ball from Igglesden into the ground and onto his stumps before he could

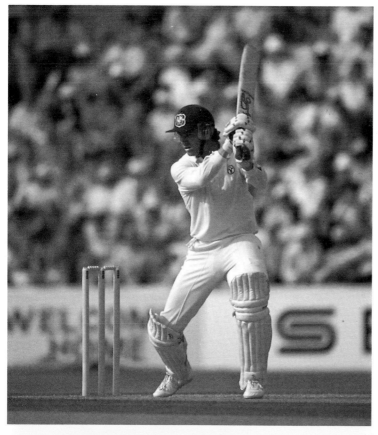

Dean Jones (LEFT) and Mark Taylor (BELOW), Australia's chief run-makers in the post-Waugh part of the series, in action in the final Test match at the Oval

LEFT Gladstone Small's batting at the Oval was a revelation

RIGHT Alan Igglesden of Kent experiences the down-side of being a Test cricketer

do any further damage, and Healy, after taking advantage, square of the wicket, of some more ill-advised bowling from Capel, had edged Pringle to Russell who took a diving catch well.

The last three wickets also went to Pringle, in the space of 19 balls, with Hughes, high in nuisance value and already slavering at the prospect of bowling on the bouncy pitch, trapped leg-before; Lawson was bowled inelegantly making room for himself, and Hohns dabbed gently to Russell once more.

But just when England were on a high, the game kicked them in the guts. Alderman's first two balls to Gooch swung away and were properly ignored by the batsman. The third jagged back, struck the front pad and up went Ken Palmer's finger. Five times now Alderman has taken a wicket in his first over; as many times, in 8 innings, Gooch has been lbw. Gooch always looks hang-dog; this time he looked dreadfully unlucky as well. A couple of minutes later came the rain.

Sixth Test, 3rd Day

Australia 468
England 124–6

In a summer where English cricket has clung desperately and pathetically to the past, it has scarcely been a surprise to look at the television screen whenever there has been a break in play, and amid groans, see Headingley and Ian Botham ad nauseam. If it has been an attempt to raise flagging English spirits, then it has failed miserably; if, on the other hand, a propaganda exercise designed to send the Aussies quaking for cover was the purpose, then it matches Neville Chamberlain half a century ago for futility.

Still, it had its interesting point, for there, rampaging in to bowl was a fresh-faced 25-year-old Australian by name of Alderman. Of course, eight years ago it was Botham and Brearley, Willis and miracles that were being fêted, but forget not as well the contribution that Alderman

made to that spectacle. Before that series, he had not played a Test; by the time the last ball had been bowled at the Oval, he had bowled 325 overs and taken a little matter of 42 wickets. No Australian before or since has taken more in an Ashes series.

By Tuesday evening, though, that, unless something unforeseen occurs, will have changed, for by taking 4 (for 34) of the six England first innings wickets that have fallen so far for 124 (still 139 short of avoiding the follow-on), Alderman has taken his tally this summer to 38. There are a possible – no probable – 14 more English wickets to fall.

The difference between the '81 Alderman and the modern version is substantial. Then, encouraged by Dennis Lillee, he lengthened his run, bowled faster and hit the seam, moving the ball off the pitch rather than in the air. Now, it's a canny bowler who shuffles more to the crease. The stiffness that will always be a legacy of the shoulder dislocation in 1982 is obvious in his careful easing overtures, although as he has five times this summer taken a wicket in his first over it does not appear to have proved too much of a handicap, the summer warmth no doubt a benefit.

'LBW Alderman' – 18 times so far, compared to 11 in all in 1981 – has, like 'caught Marsh bowled Lillee', become a cliché now, to the extent that the mode of dismissal almost seems to implant itself in the mind of umpire and player before the dismissal itself – at least that is the way it appeared when Gooch was given out by Ken Palmer on Friday. Mostly it has been achieved with away swing, at a substantially reduced pace, propelled from an arm lower than it once was, but closer to the line of the stumps because of it. Occasionally, as with Gooch, it was movement back off the seam that has done the damage. Such dismissals are always less clear cut.

There could be no brooking argument, though, with the way the England batting subsided once more in the face of Australian bowling that was competent but, given the conditions, no more than that. On the first day, pitch, light and parched outfield had been perfect for batting; by the third morning, warm and muggy under its grey duvet of cloud, the hard, bouncy surface had become a good one on which to bowl. The ball swung from the word go, not only for Alderman but for Lawson as well. Clearly, England would be in for a trying time.

Yet for 45 minutes, John Stephenson and Mike Atherton batted with a calm control that belied their inexperience. Both hit good boundaries off Lawson – Stephenson early into position to venomously pull through mid-wicket, and Atherton, timing exquisite, punching through extra cover off the back foot. Then Atherton's concentration let him down; Allan Border brought on Merv Hughes, and the young Lancastrian, a dozen to his name, drove at a wide half-volley that went a fraction wider and Ian Healy took the catch.

It brought in Robin Smith, for whom Hughes' obvious antipathy goes back to Lord's and beyond. Smith had been winning these mini-contests and crashed his first ball menacingly square. Hughes promptly let him have three rather powderpuff bouncers in a row and Dickie Bird issued a warning.

England, however, proceeded to lose half their wickets for 84 before lunch. After taking one more boundary off Hughes, Smith's stumps seemed to erupt from the earth as Lawson sneaked one between pad and bat, and then after a stay of two hours for 25, Stephenson edged Alderman to second slip. It was a worthy delivery and Stephenson had shown not only sound temperament but an ability to expand his game with attacking shots. Shortly before his dismissal, he had been struck on his unprotected forearm, which required treatment, so maybe this unsettled him. David Capel flicked his first ball from Alderman fine for four but two balls later, pushed forward down the wrong line; you can guess the rest.

Gower, meanwhile, had been doing his boy on the burning deck act, playing with a delicacy of touch and rhythmical foot movement that has not been evident since Lord's. Perhaps it's the knowledge that merciful release from a summer of torment is at hand, but until the second of two afternoon breaks for the weather proved to be the final one, he batted like an angel in making 43, with five delicious boundaries. He'd lost Jack

Scoreboard from The Oval

Australia

First Innings: 468 (M A Taylor 71, A R Border 76, D M Jones 122; D R Pringle 4 for 70).

England
First Innings

		6s	4s	Mins	Balls
G A Gooch lbw b Alderman	0	–	–	3	3
J P Stephenson c Waugh b Alderman	25	–	2	122	66
M A Atherton c Healy b Hughes	12	–	2	50	34
R A Smith b Lawson	11	–	2	19	19
*D I Gower not out	43	–	5	115	78
D J Capel lbw b Alderman	4	–	1	2	3
†R C Russell c Healy b Alderman	12	–	2	17	13
D R Pringle not out	6	–	–	45	23
Extras (lb 3, w 1, nb 7)	11				
Total (6 wkts, 38 overs)	**124**				

G C Small, A P Igglesden and N G B Cook to bat.

FALL OF WICKETS: 1–1, 2–28, 3–47, 4–80, 5–84, 6–98.

BOWLING: Alderman 14–2–34–4 (nb 10); Lawson 15–3–50–1 (w 1); Hughes 9–2–37–1 (nb 1).

Russell for 12 shortly after the lunch interval, caught behind driving at Alderman, but has so far added 26 with Derek Pringle who has been in 45 minutes for his 6.

Whether England can survive the fourth day is a moot point. The Surrey club took the opportunity earlier of distributing some T-Shirts printed with their ground sponsors named and the message 'The Final Test: August 24–29 1989'. That may prove a mite optimistic.

Sixth Test, 4th Day

Australia 468 and 87–1
England 285

It is possible – put it no higher than that – that Allan Border will become the first Australian captain to win five Test matches in a series in England. To do so, Australia will have to add a further 100 or so runs to the 270-run lead they already have, and then bowl England out in just over two sessions. Were it not for the fact that it seems to have happened already this series, such a scenario, on a pitch such as Harry Brind and his staff have produced at the Oval, would be dismissed as fantasy. It should still not happen; but avoid putting the mortgage on it just in case.

Yet in a session that has given English supporters precious little to cheer about, it is a pleasure, genuinely, to report a serious outbreak of spirit, heart and good old-fashioned backs-to-the-wall cussedness from the England lower order yesterday. Before play began, with England only four wickets left and still requiring 145 to avoid following on, it was a pound to a penny they would have been back in by tea and five down for spit by the close. Instead, the first innings was protracted by a further 54 overs, by which time the follow-on had been safely avoided and Border was obliged to cut TCCB profits by calling for the second new ball to put an end to the nonsense.

So, ladies and gentlemen, put your hands together first of all for David Gower and Derek Pringle, who took their seventh wicket stand to 71. Gower's 79, with 11 fours (not to mention a five) was a cameo of genius that ranks with anything seen this summer and transcends most, while Pringle's dogged 27, with not a single boundary to mark it, occupied $2\frac{1}{2}$ hours of Australian leisure time.

Next let's hear it for Gladstone Small and Nick Cook, who also batted for more than a couple of hours each, and finally saw England past the 269 they needed. In adding 73 for the ninth wicket, Small made 59 runs as competently as any England top order batsman could – an object lesson and inspiration for when the second innings arrives – while Cook, from the Embury school of nurdle, nudge and minimal backlift, made 31 before he was last out. For both it was their highest Test scores. England's 285, a deficit of 183, was tantamount to a triumph.

Australia needed the early breakthrough, but for once, on a morning blue and bright, but with a northern autumnal edge to the wind, neither Alderman nor Lawson was able able to find the marked movement they managed on Friday or Saturday. It was all the encouragement Gower needed. 43 overnight, and with the pitch still smooth and hard as marble, he peppered the

Scoreboard from The Oval

Australia

First Innings: 468 (M A Taylor 71, A R Border 76, D M Jones 122; D R Pringle 4 for 70).

Second Innings

	6s	4s	Mins	Balls
M A Taylor not out	43	–	6	139	110
G R Marsh lbw b Igglesden	4	–	–	16	13
D C Boon not out	29	–	3	121	93
Extras (lb 5, nb 6)	11				
Total (1 wkt, 35 overs)	**87**				

*A R Border, D M Jones, S R Waugh, †I A Healy, T V Hohns, M G Hughes, G F Lawson and T M Alderman to bat.

FALL OF WICKETS: 1–7.

BOWLING: Small 9–3–18–0; Igglesden 6–1–17–1 (nb 5); Capel 5–0–17–0; Pringle 9–0–20–0 (nb 1); Cook 6–2–10–0.

England

First Innings

	6s	4s	Mins	Balls
G A Gooch lbw b Alderman	0	–	–	3	3
J P Stephenson c Waugh b Alderman	25	–	2	122	66
M A Atherton c Healy b Hughes	12	–	2	50	34
R A Smith b Lawson	11	–	2	19	19
*D I Gower c Healy b Alderman	79	–	11	164	120
D J Capel lbw b Alderman	4	–	1	2	3
†R C Russell c Healy b Alderman	12	–	2	17	13
D R Pringle c Taylor b Hohns	27	–	–	147	90
G C Small c Jones b Lawson	59	–	8	136	97
N G B Cook c Jones b Lawson	31	–	2	123	102
A P Igglesden not out	2	–	–	38	23
Extras (b 2, lb 7, w 1, nb 13)	23				
Total (92.1 overs)	**285**				

FALL OF WICKETS: 1–1, 2–28, 3–47, 4–80, 5–84, 6–98, 7–169, 8–201, 9–274.

BOWLING: Alderman 27–7–66–5 (nb 14); Lawson 29.1–9–85–3 (w 1); Hughes 23–3–84–1 (nb 3); Hohns 10–1–30–1; Waugh 3–0–11–0.

● D I Gower's total included a five.

boundary with stroke after exquisite stroke, where the output in power belies the input in effort, apparently defying Newtonian principles; pulls swivelled to mid-wicket gave him his half-century as early as the second over of the day, another boundary went to fine leg as delicately as tickling a trout, and there were consecutive fours off Hughes, the second of which was as near vicious as Gower could get.

Pringle could only stand and admire, but alas, with exactly 100 still needed, it ended, with

Gower caught once more, by design or accident (who knows?), down the leg side, giving Alderman his sixth 5-wicket haul of the summer and his 39th wicket in all.

Good things, though, come in Small packages and Gladstone of that ilk announced himself with a cover drive off Hughes not bettered in this match, as he and Pringle embarked on a stand of 32, ended only when Border, belatedly if he had known how uncertain Pringle has looked in the past against leg spin, turned to Hohns, who immediately had Pringle taken by Taylor at slip.

Perhaps Border, with England now creeping closer, made a rare error of judgement now, for in seeking the final two wickets, he maintained his full slip cordon, leaving third man open. That, for tail enders eking out runs, can be a productive area, and so it proved. Small had launched an assault on Hohns which drove him out of the attack and Border decided to go for broke with Alderman and Hughes.

Small reached his first Test fifty from only 74 balls, and eventually it was he, turning Hughes off his legs, who took England past first base. The last two wickets fell to Lawson, with Small finally driving to cover and Cook slicing the new ball to point.

The Australian second innings that followed was once more the story of Mark Taylor. There should be a rule for him now – ask him how many runs he would settle for, give them to him and get on with the proper game. The trouble is he appears insatiable. Of Australia's 87 for one, he has so far made 43. It gives him 834 for the summer, equal with Neil Harvey as the third highest series aggregate in Test history. Only Bradman (974) and Hammond (905) are ahead of him now.

Sixth Test, 5th Day

Australia 468 and 219–4 dec.
England 285 and 143–5
Match drawn

The Ashes 1989 finally passed into history at nineteen minutes past five, when Dickie Bird and Ken Palmer, the two umpires in the final Test, met in mid-pitch, consulted their light-meters, and decided that if the batsmen so wished, play could cease forthwith. As the batsmen were the English numbers four and seven respectively, you can understand why they snaffled the opportunity like a Mark Taylor slip catch. England, with 21 overs still to bat, had made 143 for 5, still requiring 260 runs to win, and Australia were, to the bitter end, champing at the victory bit. The cloud never lifted, and shortly after six o'clock, Allan Border achieved his dearest ambition by lifting the Ashes urn – or at least a replica – aloft, just as he had watched David Gower do four years ago.

It was, in English eyes, a typically gloomy end to a gloomy series, with the day taking on an all too familiar pattern. It began with Australia at 87 for 1 in their second innings, intent on rapid progress to a declaration some time before lunch, and then a tilt at England for the rest of the day. As it happened, the declaration came during the lunch interval, at 219 for four, with England therefore needing to make 403 to win. With them not having topped 400 since the first innings of the first Test, Border seemed to be erring over-generously on the side of caution, especially as it left Australia only 67 overs in which to take 10 English wickets. Admittedly this had proved more than adequate on a number of occasions – Headingley and Trent Bridge, for example – but surely it would not be so on this delightful Test pitch.

We shall, of course, never know – the light put paid to that – but again, mercifully for the final time this season, the England batting fragmented so badly that it was only the efforts yet again of Robin Smith, who with 77 not out took his series aggregate well past 500 runs, supported by David

A thoughtful Derek Pringle on his return to Test cricket at the Oval

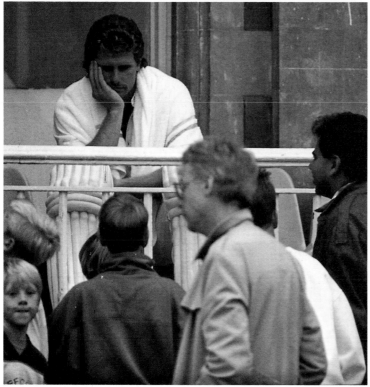

Smith must have wondered why he bothered, but his reward was to come out of the series with his Test place more secure than anyone else's

ABOVE Australian celebrations on the Oval balcony

BELOW A happy captain with his Ashes-urn replica and his XXXX

Capel, with a lesser but not insignificant 17, which pulled England from the mire. Prior to that it had been a familiar procession as Terry Alderman, the Australian man of the series (Jack Russell was England's), and Geoff Lawson cut a swathe through the England top order that left them wobbling by tea at 67 for 4.

Alderman, bowling as he had done all match from the favoured Vauxhall End, from which England lost all but three of their wickets in this match, took his total of wickets this summer to 41 – 83 in two series here, and the only bowler in history to take 40 wickets in a series twice – by dismissing John Stephenson for 11, lbw without offering a shot to a perfectly straight ball, and Graham Gooch for 10, driving a simple return catch.

Lawson then chipped in with the wickets of Mike Atherton for 14, bowled off his pad, and David Gower for 7, brilliantly caught by Steve Waugh at the finer of two gullies as he failed to keep down the last ball before tea. Atherton had batted for 64 studious minutes, but can count himself incredibly fortunate to have survived an lbw shout by Alderman before he had scored that may have been missing off and leg stumps but surely not middle!

An Australian win now looked a possibility, and it took all the fighting spirit of Smith, with dogged support from David Capel, who, with an awful lot of intimate Australian company, stayed for more than an hour, before England could consider themselves close to safety. Capel was eventually out two overs before the light closed in, caught at slip as Trevor Hohns spun a leg break across him from out of the rough created by the fast bowlers and Alderman, who received two official warnings for encroaching on the pitch, in particular.

Smith once more was superb, and it is hard to believe that had England been able to match Australia and field their absolute first choice side, he might not have made the side. Yesterday he was aided in his run-scoring by the plethora of close fielders, striking the bad ball with the ferocity and power generated by blacksmith's forearms, saving as always his greatest venom for Merv Hughes. His innings contained 11 boundaries and he dominated the fifth wicket

Scoreboard from The Oval

Australia

First Innings: 468 (M A Taylor 71, A R Border 76, D M Jones 122; D R Pringle 4 for 70).

Second Innings

	6s	4s	Mins	Balls
M A Taylor c Russell b Small	48	–	7	153	120
G R Marsh lbw b Igglesden	4	–	–	16	13
D C Boon run out (Atherton–Russell)	37	–	4	140	107
*A R Border not out	51	–	5	108	74
D M Jones b Capel	50	–	4	79	69
S R Waugh not out	7	–	–	12	12
Extras (b 2, lb 7, nb 13)	22				
Total (4 wkts dec, 63 overs)	**219**				

†I A Healy, T V Hohns, M G Hughes, G F Lawson and T M Alderman did not bat.

FALL OF WICKETS: 1–7, 2–100, 3–101, 4–189.

BOWLING: Small 20–4–57–1; Igglesden 13–1–55–1 (nb 10); Capel 8–0–35–1; Pringle 16–0–53–0 (nb 6); Cook 6–2–10–0.

England

First Innings: 285 (D I Gower 79, G C Small 59; T M Alderman 5 for 66).

Second Innings

	6s	4s	Mins	Balls
G A Gooch c and b Alderman	10	–	–	54	34
J P Stephenson lbw b Alderman	11	–	1	31	23
M A Atherton b Lawson	14	–	2	64	47
R A Smith not out	77	–	11	143	99
*D I Gower c Waugh b Lawson	7	–	–	23	24
D J Capel c Taylor b Hughes	17	–	2	66	50
†R C Russell not out	0	–	–	9	6
Extras (lb 1, w 1, nb 5)	7				
Total (5 wkts, 46.1 overs)	**143**				

D R Pringle, G C Small, A P Igglesden and N G B Cook did not bat.

FALL OF WICKETS: 1–20, 2–27, 3–51, 4–67, 5–138.

BOWLING: Alderman 13–3–30–2 (nb 3); Lawson 15.1–2–41–2 (w 1, nb 1); Hughes 8–2–34–0 (nb 2); Hohns 10–2–37–1.

Man of the Match: D M Jones (Australia).

Man of the Series: R C Russell (England) and T M Alderman (Australia).

stand of 71 with Capel, scoring all but 17 of them.

In the morning, Border had prolonged the Australian innings well beyond the time and total expected by most people. There was talk that his bowlers were the worse for flu – although any sore throats may have come through appealing – and that this might have had a bearing on the decision although later events scarcely bore this out. Mark Taylor made 48 before flashing at a wide ball from Small, David Boon was run out for 37 – just about the first mistake the Aussies have made in this department – and Dean Jones made a typically spritely half-century before getting the sort of ball from Capel that bowlers dream about and produce so rarely. There was just time for Border to complete his own fifty, from 74 balls, and that after a slow start, before lunch and the roller.

Postscript

As at Edgbaston, so at the Oval. Were it not for the substantial interference of the weather, Australia would almost certainly have won the final Test. That they did not do so in any case was due ultimately to the efforts of Gladstone Small and Nick Cook, not with the ball but with the bat, which saw England avoid the follow-on in their first innings.

In doing so, Small, a late entry into the Test and indeed the series don't forget, demonstrated a relish for the fray that has not been evident in other more experienced hands. This summer, the best English cricket has almost always come from those with nothing to lose and everything to prove: Robin Smith, plundering good competitive runs, Angus Fraser, Jack Russell and now Small.

Small, though, was in the side as a bowler and his figures did not do justice to the way he bowled. Injury notwithstanding, it is a moot point whether he has been left out in the cold for too long. His uncomplicated method, rocking and rhythmical at fast-medium with the occasional sharp delivery, has stood him in good stead against Australia in the past. It is just possible that his temperament has been found suspect when under the cosh, most notably in the final of the 1987 World Cup in the cooking pot of Eden Gardens, Calcutta, when he and DeFreitas froze and allowed Australia to get off to a winning flyer.

As an experiment and guide to the winter, the match was not a complete success. There seemed little to be gained by selecting Gooch at this stage, together with his county colleagues Stephenson and Hussain, and then omitting either of the youngsters. At least we know now that Stephenson, in spite of his excrutiatingly uncomfortable-looking stance, has the semblance of a technique, and some not-inconsiderable attacking shots, although surely no more than a number of other candidates for the opening spot. Of Hussain we are none the wiser.

Once again the Australian dominance was based on exemplary batting from Taylor (inevitably), Boon, Border, who in spite of not making a century still averaged in the 60s, and Dean Jones, whose hundred was the fastest of the series and one of the most fetching in its sheer impudence.

When you have good runs on the board, it is easier to implement pre-planned tactics and stick to them – being prepared to concede runs to third man, for example, in order to maintain a full slip cordon, is easier to rationalise if you have 500 than if things are much closer and the game is low-scoring. Border, it appeared, made this sacrifice while England were striving and getting ever closer to avoiding the follow-on. It might well have been Border's first major mistake of the summer (declaring his second innings too late was another), although he could justify both policies secure in the knowledge that whatever the outcome, it didn't really matter. Contrast this with Gower, for whom every decision had critical overtones.

How much can England positively take from the summer? To do so there has to be, and don't laugh if it seems obvious, the premise that one can look back, identify errors and learn from them. Yet the England chairman, Ted Dexter, after the match suggested neither. 'I am not aware of any errors I have made,' he said, in a display of either mega buck-passing or gross arrogance. Someone sure as hell has made some, but they are apparently not going to be identifiable because 'we do not intend to look back'. I fully understand why, after this summer, no one really wants to look back, but it's not very helpful is it?

Epilogue

Leaving the twilit Oval on Tuesday evening, ghostly empty now except for the beercan-clanking sweepers, it was hard to believe it had all been that simple. A Fawlty-ish crack of the head on the desk and we'd all wake up to find it was July, raining and England were one up going into the fourth Test.

But no, it really had been as easy as that. Four-nil brooks no argument and were it not for the weather which intervened at both Edgbaston and The Oval, it would in all probability have been the first six-nil whitewash in Test history. Allan Border and his men have done a remarkable job. If not completely unfancied – it would have been ridiculous to ignore the credentials of many of the team – most people expected the series to be closer fought than it was. But through a combination of Australian planning, skill, spirit, and exemplary leadership, and English injuries, blandness, and the legacy of a system coming home to roost, it was no contest. Some Australian players have expressed almost disappointment that things were so easy for them; in truth they loved every minute.

The triumph has been Border's, and no one would begrudge him that. Had events taken a different turn, he might have gone down as the most inept Australian captain ever; now he will be remembered as one of the best, not so much for obvious intuitive inspiration on the field like Benaud before him, say, or Brearley for England, but for the meticulous pre-planning, with Bobby Simpson, with its minute and precise attention to detail and his pragmatic, unwavering application of it on the field. Even now, I have doubts that Border as captain has the flair to change things instinctively according to the situation, but he and Simpson, utilising corporate input to the full, created a hugely effective, disciplined machine. All possible credit to them, then.

Individually, the Australians outplayed England in every department of the game except wicketkeeping, and even there Ian Healy didn't let them down, clinging on to everything that came his way, and scoring some valuable runs. The series was set up, of course, by the wonderfully consistent form of high class, technically exemplary batsmen, with five of the top six, an order unchanged throughout the series, averaging in excess of 55; only one Englishman, Robin Smith, managed that. Mark Taylor was a phenomenon – 839 runs with 2 hundreds, one a double, five fifties besides, and a lowest score of 27. That represents success beyond the dreams of anyone, and it is unlikely that Taylor will match it ever again.

Around the left-hander's steadiness, the genius of Dean Jones, Steve Waugh and Border was allowed to flourish. Waugh's first Test hundred at Headingley will live forever in the memory for its style, grace and old-time virtues; Jones's at the Oval, the last of the 11 scored in the series,

Test Averages

England

Batting and fielding

	M	I	NO	Runs	HS	100	50	Avge	Ct/St
R A Smith..........	5	10	1	553	143	2	3	61.44	1
R C Russell........	6	11	3	314	128*	1	1	39.25	14/4
D I Gower..........	6	11	0	383	106	1	2	34.81	4
J E Emburey......	3	5	1	131	64	–	1	32.75	–
K J Barnett........	3	5	0	141	80	–	1	28.20	–
N G B Cook	3	5	3	45	31	–	–	22.50	–
G R Dilley..........	2	3	1	42	24	–	–	21.00	–
B C Broad..........	2	4	0	82	37	–	–	20.50	2
G A Gooch.........	5	9	0	183	68	–	2	20.33	4
M A Atherton	2	4	0	73	47	–	–	18.25	1
N A Foster........	3	6	2	68	39	–	–	17.00	1
I T Botham.........	3	4	0	62	46	–	–	15.50	3
T S Curtis.........	3	5	0	71	41	–	–	14.20	1
D R Pringle........	2	3	0	33	27	–	–	11.00	–
P W Jarvis.........	2	3	0	33	22	–	–	11.00	–
A R C Fraser......	3	5	0	47	29	–	–	9.40	–

Played in one Test D J Capel 4, 17; P A J DeFreitas 1, 21; M W Gatting 0, 22; E E Hemmings 38, 35; A P Igglesden 2* (1 ct); A J Lamb 125, 4; D E Malcolm 9, 5; M D Moxon 0, 18; P J Newport 36, 8 (1 ct); R T Robinson 0, 12 (1 ct); G C Small 59; J P Stephenson 25, 11; C J Tavare 2.

Bowling

	O	M	R	W	Avg	Best	5WI
N A Foster.........	167	42	421	12	35.08	3.39	–
A R C Fraser......	144.2	30	323	9	35.88	4-63	–
J E Emburey.......	152	37	342	8	42.75	4-88	–
N G B Cook	103.5	23	282	5	56.40	3-91	–
D R Pringle........	86.2	12	306	5	61.20	4-70	–
G R Dilley..........	85	12	318	5	63.60	2-123	–

Also bowled: M A Atherton 8-0-34-0; K J Barnett 6-0-32-0; I T Botham 80-15-241-3; D J Capel 24-2-101-2; T S Curtis 3-0-7-0; P A J DeFreitas 63.3-10-216-3; G A Gooch 31-9-72-1; E E Hemmings 33-9-81-0; A P Igglesden 37-3-146-3; P W Jarvis 69.2-8-290-2; D E Malcolm 44-2-166-1; P J Newport 44-7-175-2; G C Small 60-12-198-4.

Australia

Batting and fielding

	M	I	NO	Runs	HS	100	50	Avg	Ct/St
S R Waugh.........	6	8	4	506	177*	2	1	126.50	4
M A Taylor........	6	11	1	839	219	2	5	83.90	5
A R Border........	6	9	3	442	80	–	6	73.66	5
D M Jones........	6	9	1	566	157	2	3	70.75	4
D C Boon..........	6	11	3	442	94	–	3	55.25	9
T V Hohns........	5	5	1	127	40	–	–	31.75	3
G R Marsh........	6	11	0	347	138	1	–	31.54	5
G F Lawson	6	5	1	115	74	–	1	28.75	–
M G Hughes	6	5	0	127	71	–	1	25.40	–
T M Alderman ...	6	4	3	20	8	–	–	20.00	2
I A Healy...........	6	7	1	103	44	–	–	17.16	14/-

Played in one Test; G D Campbell (did not bat).

Bowling

	O	M	R	W	Avg	Best	5WI
T M Alderman ...	269.2	68	712	41	17.36	6-128	6
G F Lawson	277.1	68	791	29	27.27	6-72	1
T V Hohns	134	53	300	11	27.27	3-59	–
M G Hughes	189.2	41	615	19	32.36	4-71	–

Also bowled; A R Border 24-9-44-0; G D Campbell 24-0-124-1; S R Waugh 57-15-208-2.

was a masterpiece of witty, knavish, Artful-Dodger batting.

Yet to win Tests, the opposition have to be bowled out, generally twice. So while Australia siezed control in every game by topping 400 in every one of their first innings, twice getting to 600 and once to 500, only once, in their very first efforts back at Leeds, did England manage it. Furthermore, only twice in 10 completed innings did they reach 300.

Unquestionably the man of the series was Terry Alderman, who took 41 of the 105 English

wickets to fall, through a gloriously simple expedient of keeping the ball up to the bat and bowling straight. Well, that is an over-simplification; the ball ended up straight, but described some devious routes to get there. 'LBW Alderman' should be engraved on the hearts of every English batsman, as a reminder of what a poor technique can do. Nor should one forget the contribution of Lawson, who bowled more overs than anyone and took 29 wickets. Perhaps incidentally, a special award should be made to the Australian physiotherapist for keeping these two fit.

But what of England? Luck has certainly not been kind to them – not one side originally chosen has taken the field, be it through injury or defection, and 29 players donned the lions in all. That is not a signpost to stability, and team spirit (and it presupposes anyway that the players first selected were the right ones in the first place), although it did by a happy chance lead to the discovery of Smith and Angus Fraser.

While Australia plotted and pre-planned,

England invariably acted retrospectively. So Jarvis, say, who should have played on his home ground of Headingley, was brought in to the side, in the wake of defeat, at Lord's; Fraser who might have played at Headingley as well, and certainly should have done at Lord's, had to wait until Edgbaston. Smith's chance came only because of injuries to Gatting and Lamb. English field tactics, initially strictly unenterprising and by the book, began to ape those of Australia, but whereas Border's were exact and to a purpose – the legslip to Gower, say, or the short mid-wicket to Gooch – England's were mostly arbitrary. Border maintains that you are only as good a captain as your side allows, but that is facile. He has learned from his adversity, and I'm not sure that Gower has. The acid test would be for Border and Simpson to run the England side and for Gower and Stewart to run Australia. I doubt it would have been four-nil, unless it was to England.

Yet there have been plusses for England. To discover three new players of true Test quality in a series would be a major achievement in any year, but Smith brought spirit and fight to the batting, Fraser accuracy and persistence to the bowling and Russell allied high-class, unobtrusive wicketkeeping to undreamed-of heights with the bat.

But if we can be grateful for one thing this summer, it is that the organised, technically-gifted Australians have exposed English cricket for the smug, ramshackle sham it really is. Flawed batting techniques, a product of the hurly-burly of one-day cricket and sledge-hammer bats, have been laid bare like a raw nerve; bowlers used to verdant pitches and rogue cricket balls as a substitute for skill have been found wanting against Test-class batsmen on Test surfaces. The realisation may finally have dawned that the Test side is merely the iceberg-tip: a reflection of what is going on at the sub-levels. If it results in long-term change, genuine planning with a purpose, and obliterates the notion that there is little wrong with our game that a bit of good fortune won't cure, then the humiliation won't have been entirely in vain.